THE BOTTOMLINE ON ROI

Benefits and Barriers to Measuring
Learning, Performance Improvement,
and Human Resources Programs

Patricia Pulliam Phillips

For additional copies of this publication, contact the HRDQ Client Solutions Team at:

Phone: 800-633-4533
        610-279-2002
Fax: 800-633-3683
        610-279-0524
Online: HRDQ.com

ISBN: 978-1-58854-597-8

Publisher: Martin Delahoussaye
Editorial development: Charyl Leister
Publishing assistant: Sarah Grey
Cover design: Judy Seling
Interior design: Integrative Ink

Printed in the United States of America on recycled paper.

HRDQ and the HRDQ logo are registered trademarks of Organization Design and Development, Inc.

0579E1BK

EN-01-DC-11

TABLE OF CONTENTS

THE BOTTOMLINE ON ROI

ROI INSTITUTE™

HRDQ

FOREWORD

Over the past two decades, I have had the pleasure of meeting with hundreds of executives in all types of organizations to discuss the value of various projects and programs. Executives worldwide are interested in and committed to developing their people and improving their processes. They know that a talented workforce that strives continually to improve strengthens the organization. These executives are willing to invest in processes but, as with any investment, they want to know that the investment decisions they make are the right ones—that they are successful beyond the mere activity of investing. They want to know results beyond counting activity and people. Comments such as "We have 3,000 people involved in our e-learning programs. The cost of these programs is about $11.00 per person and participants really enjoy them" are not sufficient. Executives want to see application of what people learn, behavior change, and the resulting impact these changes have on the organization, including the return on investment (ROI).

For example, results from a recent survey of CEOs from large companies that addressed their perception of the learning and development and performance improvement program investment shows that 64% of executives responding need to see application data; 96% say they want to see learning and development connected to the business impact; and 74% say they want to see ROI studies on major programs. This high level of ROI requests underscores the trend of accountability that has been working its way through the learning and development, performance improvement, and human resources fields for many years. That same survey indicates that only 11% are receiving application (behavior change) data, 8% are receiving impact data, and only 4% are receiving ROI data. More importantly, the same survey shows that 95% of these executives are directly involved in providing the funding for programs. These results reveal a gap between the data that executives receive and the data they desire.

This gap represents a challenge not only for professionals driving human performance improvement, but also for professionals performing other functions within the organization. We must meet the expectations of our principal sponsor, the person who ultimately approves our projects. Failure to do so can erode support, diminish our influence, and, yes, reduce our funding.

The Bottomline on ROI describes how to connect programs, processes, and projects to the organization in a clear, precise, and logical way. It provides the information you need to use ROI to your advantage and become an advocate of ultimate accountability.

The term ROI often inspires a variety of images and concerns. Some professionals are frightened by the notion of calculating an ROI. Anxiety ensues upon discussion of all the ways in which ROI may be interpreted and used. For those professionals who are open to learning about ROI Methodology and its benefits, however, opportunities await. ROI can be a challenge, but it can also be a tool to improve programs and projects, and provide solutions to an organization's needs. While some professionals merely debate the issue, making little progress, others are quietly and deliberately pursuing ROI in a variety of settings—and they are achieving impressive results.

ROI is not for everyone or every organization. Some organizations lack the trust and supportive climate that ROI requires. The successful champion of ROI must be willing to learn, change, and try new things—using ROI as a process improvement tool. Without this attitude and approach, it may be best not to try.

ROI is growing in prominence and popularity, and people are asking questions to decide if it is right for their organizations. Barriers to the implementation of ROI do exist, but there are ways to address and eliminate these barriers and achieve success with ROI. I have observed some realities about ROI that are often missed due to the myriad myths surrounding its use. These realities reflect the drivers behind this book and illustrate some of the challenges that an advocate will face. The stage is set for executives who can accept the realities and challenges of ROI and use it to reach their goals.

ROI Reality #1

While there are many applications and implementations of ROI, several issues inhibit the widespread use of the ROI Methodology. Although there are some realistic barriers, most of these inhibitors are myths based on misunderstandings of the process and what it can achieve.

As a tool, ROI does not currently enjoy widespread dominant application, although its use is growing steadily. Some individuals involved in ROI implementation attend ROI Certification workshops with a great deal of built-in resistance. They are driven by requests or suggestions from their senior team or by ultimatums from the top executive group. The attendees resist all the way. This is due, in part, to fear of the unknown and fear of what ROI will mean, particularly if it is negative. There is concern that a negative ROI might bring an end to their programs or their jobs. This concern is often based on misunderstanding and lack of knowledge.

This book explores and dispels the myths about ROI that challenge its use. Fear and misconception often act as barriers, but they do not have to inhibit ROI application and implementation. Some very real barriers do exist, however. The ROI Methodology will require additional time, costs, and new skills to bring change to the design, development, and implementation of programs and projects. But when considering the payoff of ROI, the benefits exceed the investment, usually by significant amounts.

ROI Reality #2

The use of ROI is client-driven, based on a quest to understand more about the ROI Methodology and its potential payoff. Prospective clients need more information on the benefits of implementing ROI.

ROI was developed in response to client needs. Senior executives of organizations pursuing ROI have asked for more detail on the business realities of ROI. They want to know the actual monetary value of the ROI Methodology so they can know, up front, what to expect in terms of payoff.

Potential clients have always addressed this issue during initial inquiries. "Show me the money," they will say. "Show me why we should pursue this. Show me the costs versus benefits so that we can make a decision." To understand what the ROI Methodology can achieve, potential users need to clarify issues, terms, and concepts that are basic to understanding the process. This book accomplishes that.

ROI Reality #3

This unique book is an indispensable guide for exploring ROI with the ultimate goal of deciding if it is right for the organization. It is a "must read" for anyone interested in ROI.

The Bottomline on ROI accomplishes several important objectives. By reading this book, the audience will gain a number of valuable benefits:

> ➤ Increase their understanding of the ROI concept, assumptions, and methodology. The book is a quick reference for the ROI Methodology.

➤ Identify who is using the ROI Methodology, why, and in what types of applications. It is important to see who is—and who is not—embracing this process improvement tool.

➤ Acquire the information necessary to make a decision about ROI. This is a critical issue. Most people explore the ROI Methodology with this question: "Is this right for us? Is this needed in our organization at this time?" This book provides the information needed to make this critical decision.

➤ Increase their appreciation of the ROI Methodology, including the vast contributions it can make. It will also help them to understand how the process has been used to add value to organizations and how it continues to add value.

➤ Reject ROI myths that get in the way of successful application and implementation.

➤ Plot their next steps. If the decision is to move forward with the process, the obvious question is, "What's next?" This book explores some of the next steps.

The Bottomline on ROI is not a detailed reference on the ROI Methodology—other books do a good job of presenting the process. This book does not dwell on case studies—others are available for that purpose. This book is not about tools, templates, and techniques—others serve as resources for application and implementation. Instead, this book enables readers to understand and make sense of the ROI Methodology from a business perspective.

ROI Reality #4

The ROI Methodology is being implemented globally in all types of organizations for all types of programs. Many professionals are using the ROI Methodology to radically change the way they design, develop, and deliver programs and solutions. These professionals represent a wide range of fields, including learning and development, organizational development, performance improvement, and human resources, along with marketing, meetings and events, and quality.

Applications of the ROI Methodology have grown significantly. Thousands of organizations in all types of settings across the globe are now using the ROI process described in this book. It is proving to be a valuable performance improvement tool, and converts are pouring in rapidly. After speaking at a conference, I overheard the training manager from a large manufacturing company make this statement: "We don't believe in ROI, and we have a policy stating we will not use ROI." Less than a year later, two individuals from the same organization attended one of our ROI Certification workshops. When I asked about their plans, they commented, "We've decided to implement the ROI Methodology throughout our learning and development organization. We have a goal to move quickly." It is not unusual to see this type of about-face. Unfortunately, too often the change is based on external pressures which have created an urgent situation.

Growth in the application of ROI has cut across all types of organizations and industries. When one major organization in an industry begins using it, others often become interested. For example, the three largest package delivery companies in the world have implemented this process, partly because their peers were using it.

The ROI Methodology has also moved into different sectors. It began primarily in the manufacturing sector—the logical birthplace of any process improvement tool. It quickly moved to the service sector, then to non-profits and healthcare, and on to government and non-governmental organizations. We are now beginning to see applications in the education sector, as schools and universities struggle to show the value of their programs.

While the process was initially employed to show the impact of supervisor training, now it is used in all types of programs, from highly technical programs to long-term executive development. Applications include coaching and management development programs, such as business coaching, mentoring, career development, and succession planning. Human resource programs—such as orientation, compensation systems, recruiting strategies, employee relations initiatives, and retention solutions—are also being evaluated successfully using the ROI Methodology.

ROI Reality #5

Sooner or later, every function will face increasing accountability and will have to address ROI. For some, the time is now. For others it may be long-term, but it will eventually surface.

Many important influences are responsible for the growth in use of ROI. Four of those influences are emphasized here:

1. Global economic forces are making it necessary for all segments of an organization to show the payoff of all programs, projects, and solutions. Every function must make a contribution.

2. ROI is the ultimate level of evaluation, where the cost of the solution is compared to its monetary benefits. While other levels of evaluation are important, nothing tells the story quite like ROI, particularly for those sponsors and clients demanding a monetary payback.

3. The ROI concept is familiar to most managers, particularly those with business school degrees. They see it as an important accountability tool. They have seen it applied in other areas and welcome its use with processes such as learning and development, performance improvement, and human resources. They realize that it is not a fad—it is a proven technique that will exist for years to come.

4. Top executives are requiring this type of measurement for new (and existing) programs. Previously, they hesitated to ask for ROI because they did not realize it could be applied to so many areas. In some situations, they were told it is impossible to measure ROI for programs such as learning, human resources, and

other "soft issues." Now that they realize that it *can* be done, they are requiring this level of evaluation.

ROI Reality #6

A new breed of performance improvement executive is achieving success with ROI. These executives are using the ROI Methodology to show value as they operate with a business mindset. They are becoming business partners with the front line of the organization.

The good news: change and success are occurring. A new breed of executive is managing many support functions, such as learning and development, performance improvement, and human resources. These new executives bring a business mindset to the table. They want to operate these functions as important business enterprises, as major contributors, adding value to the business—using the ROI Methodology to support the cause.

These new executives are choosing to be proactive instead of reactive when it comes to implementing the ROI Methodology. They realize that they must take the lead and facilitate change or it will not happen. ROI is being recognized as a necessary tool. In any functional part of a business, performance must be validated if that functional part is to be recognized as a contributor.

Finally, this new breed of executive sees ROI as a challenge. It is not a quick fix. Application of this process to all of the different situations, scenarios, and environments is complex. Executives understand that change is a process that requires learning, unlearning, and relearning. The best processes move quickly, then stall and even relapse, but it is by overcoming the good, the bad, and the ugly that functions can adjust, change, and implement successful, sustainable ROI practices.

Patti, author of this book, my business partner, and my wife, has experience in a large corporation, which positions her to understand the uniqueness of support functions as well as their particular need to show value. When she first became aware of the ROI Methodology, the overwhelming need for its use in functions such as learning and development, human resources, and marketing was evident. She embraced the process, quickly realized why others were interested, and saw what they needed to help them move along the way.

Patti is an astute observer of the ROI Methodology, building her expertise from literally hundreds of presentations, consulting assignments, and engagements. She is an excellent researcher and teacher of the process—studying how it is developed and explaining how it works. She has become the top ROI expert. She brings a unique perspective—not as the individual who initially developed the process for applications in learning and development, but as a person who has observed it, has applied it successfully, and now lives with it in every way. I think that you will enjoy this book.

Jack J. Phillips
Developer of the ROI Methodology
Chairman and Co-Founder, ROI Institute, Inc.

INTRODUCTION

C onsider the scenario below:
 Sydney Mitchell has been serving as CEO for Global
Communications for the past nine months. She has a reputation
for being aggressive in meeting goals, yet is pragmatic and fair.
In her previous organization, Sydney increased profits as well as
customer satisfaction ratings while reducing staff and position-
ing the company as one of the 100 best companies to work for.
Before making significant changes in Global Communications's
organizational structure, Sydney is giving each function one year
to make strides toward meeting strategic objectives. These strategic objectives focus on increasing profits, market share, customer
satisfaction ratings, and employee satisfaction ratings. Sydney has
communicated these objectives very clearly during her first nine
months and even holds monthly learning sessions with employees,
team leaders, and executives to help them understand the meaning
and importance of each objective.

 With three months remaining in the year, Sydney is in another
round of meetings with the executives of each function to get status reports. She has been relatively pleased with the results in the marketing,
human resources, and distribution functions. Today she is meeting with
the President of GlobalCom University, Global Communications's
corporate university.

 Donald Hodges is the President of GlobalCom University. He was
hand-picked by the past CEO and believes that the university is making a difference. He always receives rave reviews from participants after
each program. Donald is ready for Sydney. He has a flashy PowerPoint

presentation, and the results of all of his program evaluations are ready to review.

Sydney enters the room.

Sydney: Hi, Donald. It's nice to see you. The place looks great and everyone seems really busy.

Donald: Yes, Sydney. We're developing 12 new programs.

Sydney: Really? What are these programs?

Donald: Well, we're developing a new communications program, as well as revising our orientation program to include our new benefits package. We've also had requests from employees to offer programs they're interested in, including a dress-for-success program, a time management program, and a business etiquette program. And we're developing a leadership program similar to one that I attended recently and really enjoyed. I think the managers will enjoy it as well.

Sydney: Hmmmmm. How much time does it take to develop these programs?

Donald: Oh, not long; about a week for each day of training at the most. We have our four program developers working on three programs each. I estimate it will take a few months to develop all 12 programs.

Sydney: I see. A few months…

Donald: Come on into the conference room, Sydney. I want to share our accomplishments thus far!

Sydney: Great, I'd really like to see.

Donald boots up the presentation. He goes through all the preliminary issues, and then gets to the results of the past nine months.

Donald: In the past nine months we have developed 10 new programs, offered 1,724 hours of training, had 3,680 employees attend training, and received an average of 4.5 out of 5 on the program satisfaction rating. So basically, we have developed new training, offered some of the new programs as well as some of the old favorites, and the employees attending training seem to think we're moving in the right direction.

Sydney: Thanks for the update, Donald. Do we know about the success of these programs on the job?

Donald: No, not specifically, but we are confident that they are adding value.

Sydney: How do you know you're adding value?

Donald: Because of the feedback we receive.

Sydney: What kind of feedback do you receive?

Donald: Many of the participants tell us that they have been very successful with what they have learned.

Sydney: So, you've actually had a follow-up after each program?

Donald: No, not exactly. We just receive random comments.

Sydney: So you have no organized way of knowing about the success of your programs?

Donald: Well, it's not a formal follow-up, but we still receive good feedback.

Sydney: I see. Well, thanks, Donald. I'd like to meet with you next Monday to discuss your contribution to the organization.

Put yourself in Donald's position. How do you think the meeting went? Now, put yourself in Sydney's position. Does Donald demonstrate value for the corporate university? Did he show how programs connect with profit or market share? Did he make connections with measures of customer satisfaction or employee satisfaction? What will be the fate of GlobalCom University?

All too often this same scenario plays out in organization after organization. Program and project owners are excited about the activity around what they do. And it is this activity that often provides the basis for decisions about programs—decisions that often result in smaller budgets, fewer staff, less status, more skepticism, and growing frustration for everyone. Activity does not translate to results. Activity, while necessary to get the job done, represents costs. Costs get cut. Results, however, reflect the benefits of an investment. Investments are allocated. Learning and development, performance improvement, human resources, and other functions that support the business within an organization are shifting from an activity-based paradigm to a results-based paradigm.

From Activity to Results

For decades, senior leaders accepted many processes, such as learning and development and human resources, as necessary costs to ensure that the human side of the organization remained intact and well-trained. Billions of dollars were spent on developing people but few questions were asked. Activity-based organizations implemented programs without a clearly defined business need or an assessment of the performance issues driving the business need. They failed to set specific measurable objectives to position programs for results. In addition, they failed to prepare participants to achieve results. Activity-focused organizations did not make an effort to prepare the work environment to support transfer of knowledge, skill, and information to actual performance. Programs moved forward without plans to ensure that success would occur after content was disseminated. Organizations that focused solely on activity made little, if any, effort to build partnerships with key managers, and they neglected to measure results in terms that resonated with key managers and executives, including the cost-benefit comparison. Activity-focused organizations placed emphasis on inputs rather than outcomes. But today, things have changed.

Today, senior leaders are asking questions. They want to know what value investing in initiatives brings to the organization. They want to know the business impact of programs and projects as well as the ROI. Many organizations are heeding these demands by focusing their efforts on results.

Results-based organizations ensure that programs link to specific business measures and that the assessment of performance effectiveness occurs so that, given the business needs, the right performance is addressed. Specific, measurable objectives for behavior change and business impact are developed routinely. These objectives are communicated to participants to prepare them to achieve results and to position the programs for success. In addition, results-based organizations prepare the environment for knowledge transfer by developing transfer strategies, describing who needs to do what and when they need to do it in order to put knowledge, skill, and information acquisition to use. Partnerships with key managers and clients exist in results-based organizations, and measures are taken to ensure that programs and projects are achieving the results important to these partners. Finally, results-based organizations plan for and report outputs and outcomes, and answer the basic question, "So what?"

Many of these results-based organizations have adopted the ROI Methodology described in this book. While the adoption of such a process does not cause an immediate shift from one extreme of the Activity–Results continuum to the other, methodical, systematic implementation does enable an organization to move toward a results-based paradigm. Over the past few decades, the ROI process has been vastly successful in helping leaders and professionals address their accountability needs, describe program results in terms that resonate with all stakeholders, and provide data useful in making improvements to all types of programs. Thousands of individuals have been trained in the process and hundreds of organizations in over 50 countries are applying it. So, why does it work for so many organizations?

Why the ROI Methodology Works

The ROI Methodology presents a balanced set of measures. ROI is the ultimate measure of success given that it requires that both program benefits and costs be converted to money so that a direct comparison can be made; however, it is not the only measure of success. Additional measures provide a more complete story of program success and help to explain how the ROI is developed. In order to develop this balanced set of measures, a process must be put in place. The ROI Methodology provides this process. Step by step, program owners and evaluators can conduct comprehensive ROI studies while ensuring consistency in their approach. Through the use of standards, or guiding principles, the process can be replicated time and time again.

The ROI Methodology balances research and statistical methods with practical application. Fundamental research principles are always followed, but programs and processes are not researched to no end. Organizations need data and they need it quickly, so a balance occurs between how much to invest in an evaluation and the value of the data evolving from it.

A process must be scalable, meaning that if it works for one function it should work for another. The ROI Methodology is scalable. Organizations applying it in learning, human resources, and performance improvement often expand its use to other functions such as marketing, meetings and events, and quality. This scalability allows programs of all types to be evaluated using the same process, thereby developing results that can actually be compared.

Probably the most important aspect of the ROI Methodology is that it is credible to senior managers. The ROI metric is familiar to accountants and financiers in all organizations. It is fundamental. In addition, senior leaders can easily see how the connection between a program and its results transpires. They also appreciate the conservative approach required by the ROI Methodology, which guarantees that the ROI is understated rather than inflated.

About this Book

In 2002, Jack Phillips let me boil down his life's work to 99 pages. The first edition of *The Bottomline on ROI* was awarded the 2003

International Society for Performance Improvement (ISPI) Award of Excellence for Outstanding Instructional. Communication, an honor of which both Jack and I are very proud. The book reviews were good and many people wrote or commented that the book provided a good overview of a complex topic. This feedback provided an indication that the book achieved its objective: to provide a simple but direct overview of the ROI Methodology to help readers decide whether or not they want to pursue the process further.

Since 2002, the application of the ROI Methodology has expanded exponentially. While the foundation of our work is still learning and development, performance improvement, and human resources, we've moved into other areas. Professionals in the meetings and events, rewards and recognition, and marketing industries are embracing ROI as a tool to show value for their efforts. Organizations striving to contribute to the green movement while contributing to the bottomline are using the ROI Methodology. We are probably most proud of our efforts to help organizations whose missions are to serve society at large build capacity in the ROI Methodology. Our ROI Certification program is on the course agenda of the United Nations System Staff College, Turin, Italy, where we teach the ROI Methodology to staff from UN agencies serving missions around the world.

The topic of ROI continues to appear in books, on conference agendas, and in trade publications. Even with its growth and acceptance, the topic still stirs up emotions. Some individuals characterize ROI as inappropriate for programs such as learning, performance improvement, and human resources while others passionately characterize ROI as the answer to their accountability concerns. The truth lies somewhere between these viewpoints.

The Bottomline on ROI presents the rationale for developing and implementing a comprehensive measurement and evaluation process that includes ROI. The book presents and explores an evaluation process that is credible to key stakeholders. Implementing the ROI Methodology generates a scorecard of balanced measures including participant reaction, satisfaction, and planned action; learning; application; impact; ROI; and intangible benefits. This scorecard provides a clear indication of the actual impact of programs, processes, and initiatives.

Whether seeking an initial understanding of ROI evaluation or looking for ways to generate support for ROI within an organization, this book provides readers with a fundamental understanding of ROI and how it can be implemented. Included in this book are the following:

- Key issues driving the need to measure programs and projects

- Benefits of developing ROI

- Profile of typical organizations that are using ROI

- Symptoms indicating that an organization is ready for ROI

- Pieces of the evaluation puzzle necessary to build a comprehensive measurement and evaluation system

- Criteria for effective ROI implementation

- The ROI Methodology model that will produce a balanced set of measures

- A communication process model for ensuring effective communication both during and after the process

- Steps to get started implementing the ROI Methodology

This second edition also includes answers to the 25 most frequently asked questions about ROI. These answers can be found in Chapter 6.

How to Get the Most of this Book

This book was written to serve as a primer to ROI. You will not find detailed steps and calculations in this book. You will find, however, enough information to acquire a basic understanding of the ROI Methodology. This book can be used for the following purposes:

- Learning the basics of ROI

- Providing an overview of ROI to team members

- Persuading managers that ROI is the right choice for your organization

- Beginning to develop your measurement and evaluation strategy

After reading the book, you may want answers to additional questions about ROI and how it will serve your needs. You can find these answers through various workshops and resources described in the back of the book. If after reading the book you are interested in sharing the process with your team, purchase the entire tool kit for every member. For the first time, we at the ROI Institute have created a Participant Workbook so that organizations can build capacity in the basics of ROI on their own. We have even developed a Facilitator Guide to help you to teach the process to your team. Details on this opportunity are provided in the back of the book.

Acknowledgments

No project is the work of just one individual. First, thanks go to CEP Press for publishing the first edition of the book, and for turning over the copyright to me so that I can use the content as needed, including publishing a second edition.

Many thanks go to Martin Delahoussaye, Vice President of Publishing at HRDQ, for taking on the project. We know that by collaborating with HRDQ on this book we can help organizations to gain a better understanding of what ROI is, what it is not, and how the ROI Methodology can position their programs for success.

As with all of our projects, special thanks go to the team at the ROI Institute. Particular thanks go to Mary Beth and Linda for holding down the fort as Jack and I travel the world spreading the ROI word. You are much appreciated.

Finally, thanks go to Jack for the work he has done and for the way in which he allows others to take his work and run with it. Your passion for your work and your need to continue striving for perfection are inspiring. If only we all had your energy! Thank you for being my biggest fan and for supporting me in all my efforts.

CHAPTER 1: ROI DEFINED

The issue of ROI (return on investment) and its use continues to grow in prominence. ROI appears in books, on conference agendas, and in promotional and advertising materials. Rarely does a topic stir up emotions to the degree the ROI issue does. But just what is ROI?

The ROI Calculation

ROI is a financial metric describing the return on investment in a program, process, or initiative. It compares the monetary benefits of an investment to the investment itself. ROI is considered the ultimate measure of program success for a variety of reasons, one of which is that it requires normalizing program benefits and costs through the use of money so that the two can be equally compared. In this one metric, economic contribution is apparent. The concept of return on investment ROI has been used for centuries (Sibbett 1997) and this single statistic can be compared to other opportunities inside or outside the company. There are several metrics that compare the financial benefits of an investment to the cost. Most often used for programs such as learning and development, performance improvement, and human resources are the benefit-cost ratio (BCR) and the ROI percentage. Occasionally a payback period may be calculated and, for capital investments, the net present value (NPV) is often used.

Benefit-Cost Ratio (BCR)

The benefit-cost ratio is one of the oldest measures of return on investment. An output of cost-benefit analysis, the BCR compares the monetary benefits of an investment to the cost, resulting in a ratio. Grounded in welfare economics and public finance, cost-benefit analysis has historically served as a feasibility tool to justify government involvement in the economy and to examine the extent of government's influence on the private sector and on the welfare of society at large (Thompson 1980; Kearsley 1982; Nas 1996; Phillips 1997b).

In formula form, the following is the BCR:

$$BCR = \frac{\textbf{Benefits}}{\textbf{Costs}}$$

The following steps lead to the BCR:

- Identify the annual benefits or gains from implementing a program

- Convert benefits to monetary value using either profit, cost savings, or cost avoidance associated with the investment

- Determine the cost (or investment) of the program

- Identify the intangible benefits of program implementation

- Compare the monetary benefits to the program costs

- Compare the result to some alternative program or a standard for acceptance

Reported as a ratio, the BCR describes how the annual monetary benefits returned compare to the cost. For example, if a program returns $650,000 in monetary benefits from profit, cost savings, and/or cost avoidance over a one-year period and costs the organization $350,000, the BCR is this:

$$BCR = \frac{\$650,000}{\$350,000} = 1.86:1$$

This BCR indicates that for every $1 invested in the program, $1.86 is returned. The classic decision-making criterion for the BCR is that anything over a 1:1 BCR is acceptable.

Return on Investment (ROI)

Return on investment is the ultimate measure of the profitability of an investment and is the classic tool used to report this profitability. Applied for centuries by financiers, the metric became widespread in the 1960s for measuring operating performance in industry (Horngren 1982). Today, this simple metric is standard in business and is now used in non-business settings when reporting the economic contribution of all types of investments.

BCR was historically used as a feasibility tool in deciding whether or not to move forward on projects. ROI was a measure of past performance, basing assumptions on historical data. Today, ROI is commonly developed up front to forecast benefits and is used to make investment decisions, whereas BCR is now commonly used as a post-investment measure of actual results. ROI compares annual earnings (or net program benefits) to the investment (or program costs). Unlike its cousin BCR, ROI is reported as a percentage and represents the annual *net* benefits returned over and beyond the initial investment. The steps used to develop the data necessary to calculate the ROI are similar to those used to calculate the BCR; however, the difference is in the way the return is calculated, as shown in the following equation:

$$ROI = \frac{\textbf{Net Benefits}}{\textbf{Costs}} \times 100$$

Using the earlier example, for a program achieving $650,000 in monetary benefits and requiring an investment of $350,000, the ROI is this:

$$ROI = \frac{\$650,000 - \$350,000}{\$350,000} \times 100 = 86\%$$

The resulting ROI explains that for every $1 invested in the program, that dollar is returned plus a gain of 86 cents ($0.86). The 86 cents represents the *return* on the investment. While this seems like a reasonable return, acceptance of an 86% ROI is dependent on the standard to which this ROI is compared.

What makes a good ROI?

An ROI is only as good as that to which it is compared. Use the following guidelines to help you establish your target ROI.

- Set the ROI at the same level as other investments, e.g., 18%
- Set the ROI slightly higher than the level of other investments, e.g., 25%
- Set the ROI at break-even, 0%
- Ask the client to help set the target ROI

Payback Period (PP)

Periodically, it may be useful to estimate the time at which an investment will pay back. This payback period is calculated by comparing the initial investment with the annual cash flows or monetary benefits due to the program. The equation is simply a reverse of the BCR.

Payback period is reported in terms of number of months or years. Using the earlier example, the payback period for a program reaping $650,000 in monetary benefits and costing the organization $350,000 is this:

$$PP = \frac{\$350,000}{\$650,000} = .54$$

By multiplying .54 by 12 months, we arrive at a payback period for this program of 6.48 months. This tells decision makers they can expect to recover their investment in less than one year. This payback period is compared to that of other potential investments or to a predetermined standard.

ROI, BCR, and PP are appropriate when comparing the monetary benefits of investing in programs targeting human resources and the development of those resources. While people are assets to an organization, they are not treated the same way in the accounting books as other assets, such as equipment, land, and buildings. Also, many people-focused initiatives are short-term in nature, meaning that they take only a few months, weeks, or even days to fully implement. Bearing this in mind, it is important to remember that a payoff within the first year of such an investment is desirable, if not required (Phillips and Phillips 2007).

Net Present Value (NPV)

Because the issue often comes up in ROI discussions, it is important to note a commonly used technique in making capital budgeting decisions—net present value. NPV is one of several discounted cash flow (DCF) methods that account for the time-value of money and are used for long-range decisions.

Using NPV, expected cash inflows (program benefits) and outflows (program costs) are discounted to the present value at a given point in time, using a preselected discount rate. The assumed benefits over a period of time (discounted at the determined discount rate) are added together and the initial investment is subtracted. The future benefits and costs are reduced to a single present dollar value. If the present value of benefits is greater than the investment, the program is assumed to be a good investment (Nas 1996; Friedlob and Plewa 1996).

DCF methods are useful if one is investing in technology, has large capital expenses for which a constant stream of benefits is ensured, or if one is investing today for some future realized return. For non-capital expenditures or programs that are considered short-term but from which benefits are expected in the near-term, however, DCF methods are not appropriate.

Other Measures of Financial Return

ROI is the topic of many a conversation. It is good news that the conversation is taking place, particularly in areas where ROI has not historically been a consideration. The bad news, however, is that these conversations sometimes lead to the creation of creative, albeit meaningless, spins on various financial acronyms. Take for example, ROE, which, from a business perspective, is defined as return on equity. Return on equity is determined by comparing net income to share-holders' equity. ROE is useful for comparing the profitability of a given company to that of other firms in the same industry. It is not a measure suitable for valuing investment in people, processes, and projects. Unfortunately, when I asked an audience of learning and performance improvement professionals how they defined ROE, they responded, "Return on Expectations." While the acronym is clever, it is meaningless in terms of measures of economic contribution. It is important that professionals at all levels and in all functions of an organization at least recognize the difference between what is merely clever and what is meaningful from a business perspective. Table 1 presents a brief list of acronyms representing key financial measures and their associated definitions.

Table 1. Financial Measures

Acronym	Definition	Description
ROI	Return on Investment	Used to evaluate the efficiency or profitability of an investment or to compare the efficiency of a number of investments. Calculation: Compares the annual net benefits of an investment to the cost of the investment, expressed as a percentage. ROI = (Net Benefits/Costs) × 100
ROE	Return on Equity	Measures a corporation's profitability by revealing how much profit a company generates with the money that shareholders have invested. Used for comparing the profitability of a company to that of other firms in the same industry. Calculation: Compares the annual net income to shareholder equity. ROE = Net Income/Shareholder Equity
ROA	Return on Assets	Indicates how profitable a company is in relation to its total assets. Measures how efficient management is at using its assets to generate earnings. Calculation: Compares annual net income (annual earnings) to total assets, expressed as a percentage. ROA = Net Income/Total Assets
ROAE	Return on Average Equity	Modified version of ROA referring to a company's performance over a fiscal year. Calculation: Same as ROA except the denominator is changed from total assets to average shareholders' equity, which is computed as the sum of the equity value at the beginning and end of the year divided by two. ROAE = Net Income/Average Shareholder Equity

Acronym	Definition	Description
ROCE	Return on Capital Employed	Indicates the efficiency and profitability of a company's capital investments. ROCE should always be higher than the rate at which the company borrows; otherwise any increase in borrowing will reduce shareholders' earnings. Calculation: Compares earnings before interest and tax (EBIT) to total assets – current liabilities. ROCE = EBIT/Total Assets – Current Liabilities
PV	Present Value	Current worth of a future sum of money or stream of cash flows (C) given a specified rate of return. Important in financial calculations including net present value, bond yields, pension obligations. Calculation: Divides amount of cash flows (or sum of money) by the interest rate over a period of time. $PV = C/(1+r)^t$
NPV	Net Present Value	Measures the difference between the present value of cash inflows and the present value of cash outflows. Another way to put it: measures the present value of future benefits with the present value of the investment. Calculation: Compares the value of a dollar today to the value of that same dollar in the future, taking into account a specified interest rate over a specified period of time. $NPV = \sum_{t-1}^{T} (C_t/(1+r)^t) - C_0$
IRR	Internal Rate of Return	Makes the net present value of all cash flows from a particular project equal to zero. Used in capital budgeting. The higher the IRR, the more desirable it is to undertake the process. Calculation: Follows the NPV calculation as a function of the rate of return. A rate of return for which this function is zero is the internal rate of return. $NPV = \sum_{n=0}^{N} (C_n/(1+r)^n) = 0$

Acronym	Definition	Description
PP	Payback Period	Measures the length of time to recover an investment. Calculation: Compares the cost of a project to the annual benefits or annual cash inflows. PP = Costs/Benefits
BCR	Benefit-Cost Ratio	Used to evaluate potential costs and benefits of a project that may be generated if the project is completed. Used to determine financial feasibility. Calculation: Compares project annual benefits to its cost. BCR = Benefits/Costs

Imperfection of Financial Measures

Regardless of the ROI metric used, the calculation alone is an imperfect measurement that must be used in conjunction with other performance measures as part of a measurement and evaluation process (Horngren 1982). Reporting a single financial metric provides evidence of success in terms of what that measure means, but that single measure doesn't tell the whole story. For example, a learning and development function evaluates a performance management program for new store managers. The ROI is 75%. Senior managers ask these questions:

- Is that good? How do you know?

- How did you arrive at 75% ROI?

- Who was involved in the program?

- What prevented you from getting a higher return?

- Can you improve it?

- How do you know that ROI is due to your program and not the new technology employed in the stores?

Without additional data, the story is limited to economics only. Other measures of success tell the rest of the ROI story. These measures include the following:

- Inputs into the process, including target audience, number of people, and cost per person. These measures represent the scope of the program.

- Participants' reaction to the program, particularly their perception of the relevance of the program's content, the importance the content will have to their jobs, and their intent to apply what they learned in the program. These measures of utility can often provide predictive information regarding the learning and application of the skills (Alliger and Tannenbaum 1997; Warr, Allan, and Birdi 1999; APQC 2000).

- The extent to which learning can be applied immediately following the program so that the application of the new knowledge, skills, and information becomes routine.

- The extent to which new knowledge, skills, and information are applied in order to improve key business measures. In addition, data around how the organization's system supports learning transfer and what barriers might prohibit participants from applying what they learn.

- The improvement in business measures as a result of the application of new knowledge, skills, and information learned in the program. Further, how the improvement is connected to the program versus other influencing factors.

These data explain how the ROI is derived and provide information necessary to improve the program and the system that supports learning transfer.

Rationale for Implementing ROI

Programs, processes, and projects are implemented routinely throughout all types of organizations, but as the costs of these programs escalate, the budgets for these initiatives become targets for others who would like to divert the money to their own projects. The learning and development industry spends billions of dollars annually. ASTD estimates that U.S. organizations spent $125.9 billion in employee learning in 2009 (ASTD, 2010). This excludes the billions spent outside the United States. That is enormous, especially considering that research shows anywhere from 38 to 50 percent of new learning content is not transferred to the job.

Along with the fact that costs are rising, there are other specific issues driving the current need to measure the results of learning and development, performance improvement, and human resources programs.

Consequences of Ineffective Programs

Ineffective programs bring additional scrutiny and skepticism to bear on all functions within the organization. Many programs do not live up to their promises or expectations. They do not deliver the expected results—at least not in terms the client understands. When results are insufficient, concern often surrounds the credibility of the evaluation process, the program, and the overall function. As a result, greater constraints and demands are placed on the function. In many cases, the consequences of ineffective practices lead to restructuring, elimination of processes, and sometimes the displacement of staff members. By implementing a sound ROI Methodology, organizations can weed out ineffective programs or make existing programs more effective.

Linking to Strategic Initiatives

The need to link processes to the strategic direction of the company applies to all functions—including those focused on employee development and performance. The importance of linking programs to organizational strategy is another major reason to pursue a comprehensive measurement and evaluation process. Management often scrutinizes programs to determine what value they bring to the overall strategy. How do they fit? How will they help the organization to achieve its goal? Are the right programs being offered and, if so, how do we know? The need to link programs to the organization's strategic objectives and report results that reflect these objectives brings a greater interest in the accountability of such programs and drives the need for ROI.

At-Risk Funding

Some organizations put resources at risk by basing the allocation of resources on the actual monetary contribution of programs (Schmidt 1997). For example, annual budgets are placed at risk by basing them on a threshold ROI. If the minimum ROI is met for key programs, the budget remains level. Exceeding the threshold results in increased budget; falling below the threshold causes a reduction of budget. This pay-for-performance process requires the use of an ROI process that ensures credible, reliable results.

Top Executive Requirements

Increased interest in ROI from the executive suite is becoming commonplace in organizations in the United States as well as other countries around the world. Top executives who have watched their budgets grow without appropriate accountability measures are becoming frustrated, and, in an attempt to respond to the situation, they are demanding a return on investment for these programs. Executives have to make appropriate funding decisions based on the impact programs have on the financial health of their organizations. Without a measure that can be compared across all programs and processes, decisions are often based on perception or political interest. Managers and staff must show evidence of program impact using a measure that is compatible with those used in other operational elements so that top executives can operate the organization effectively.

The Need for Balanced Measures

There is continuous debate as to what should or should not be measured and which results provide the best evidence of program impact. Some prefer soft measures obtained directly from clients and consumers, such as work habits, work climate, and attitudes. Others prefer hard data focused on key issues of output, quality, cost, and time. A better system employs a balanced set of measures that takes into consideration participant preferences, learning, application, change in business measures, the actual ROI, and intangible measures. Data should be examined from a variety of sources, at different time periods, and for different purposes. The need for balanced measures is a major driver of the ROI Methodology in that it provides financial impact (ROI) along with the other important measures.

Desire to Contribute

Individuals engaged in professional work want to know that their efforts make a difference. They need to see that they are making a contribution in terms that managers and executives respect and appreciate. One of the most self-satisfying elements of program ownership may be showing the ROI of key programs. A comprehensive measurement and evaluation process not only shows the success of a program in terms of schedule, budget, and client feedback, but also reflects the actual monetary value added. An impressive ROI provides the final touch to a major program. This type of evaluation serves as evidence for staff, managers, and executives that programs of all types do make a difference.

Benefits of the ROI Methodology

Routine use of the ROI Methodology can generate several specific benefits. Collectively, these benefits add enough value to develop a positive ROI on implementing the ROI Methodology.

Show the Contribution of Selected Programs

With ROI, both the client and the staff will know the specific contribution of a program. The ROI calculation will show the actual net benefits versus the cost, elevating the evaluation data to a clear level of accountability. This process presents indisputable evidence of program success. When a program succeeds, in many cases the same type of program can be applied to other areas in the organization. Thus, if one division has success with a program and another division has the same needs, the program may add the same value to that division, enhancing the overall success of all programs.

Earn the Respect of Senior Management

Demonstrating the impact of programs is one of the most convincing ways to earn the respect and support of the senior management team—and not just for one particular program. Managers respect processes and programs that add bottomline value in terms they understand. ROI evaluation is comprehensive; when applied consistently to several programs it can convince management that all functions are important investments, not just costs. Mid-level managers will view programs and projects as making a viable contribution to their immediate objectives. ROI is a critical step toward helping leaders and staff to build successful partnerships with the senior management team.

Gain the Confidence of Clients

Evaluation using the ROI Methodology provides clients—those requesting and authorizing programs—a complete set of data to show the overall success of a program. Providing both qualitative and quantitative data, the balanced profile of results from the ROI Methodology provides coverage from different sources, at different time frames, and with different types of data. Implementing the ROI Methodology provides the information needed to validate the initial decision to move forward with a new program, continue an existing program, or eliminate an ineffective program.

Improve Processes

Because a variety of feedback data is collected during the evaluation of a program, comprehensive analysis provides data to drive process changes. The data allow program owners to make adjustments during program implementation. Data also help to improve future programs by identifying which processes are nonproductive and which add value. Thus, ROI evaluation becomes an important process improvement tool both during and after a program.

Develop a Results-Based Approach

The entire process of ROI evaluation requires that all stakeholders be involved, including program designers and developers, facilitators, and evaluators. Throughout program design and implementation, the entire team of stakeholders focuses on results. From detailed planning to the actual communication of results, every team member has a responsibility to achieve success. This focus often enhances the evaluation results because the ultimate outcomes are clearly in mind. In essence, the program begins with the end in mind. Program processes, activities, and steps focus on evaluation measures, from how well participants respond to the program to the actual ROI. As the function demonstrates success, confidence grows, enhancing the results of future program evaluations.

Alter or Eliminate Ineffective Programs

If a program is not going well and the expected results are not materializing, data from ROI will prompt changes or modifications to the program. These changes can take place during program implementation so that the final results are positive, or changes can take place in between program offerings based on the results of comprehensive evaluation. When an organization stays on track with the evaluation process, programs can evolve continuously so as to enhance overall results. On the other hand, a comprehensive ROI evaluation can provide evidence that the program will not achieve desired results. While it takes courage to eliminate a program, in the long term, this action will reap important benefits.

ROI on the ROI

Most organizations spend less than 1 percent of their direct budgets on measurement and evaluation processes. This figure considers only the post-program analysis or comprehensive review process. Interjecting accountability throughout a program requires expenditures closer to 3–5 percent of the total budget. Use of the ROI Methodology will generate specific, measurable savings to offset this expenditure. Among these are the following:

- Preventing the implementation of unnecessary programs (after an evaluation of a pilot indicates that a program will not add value)

- Altering or redesigning existing programs to make them more effective (and less expensive)

- Eliminating unproductive and ineffective programs (thus eliminating their costs)

- Expanding the implementation of successful programs (adding value to other divisions, regions, etc.)

Many organizations keep a running total of the monetary benefits derived from implementing an ROI Methodology. In comparing these benefits to the cost of implementation, the results yield a positive "ROI on the ROI."

Candidates for ROI

Accountability does not apply to just one particular type of organization. Bringing accountability to programs and processes is a basic concern for organizations regardless of their product, service, mission, or scope. Accountability issues exist in organizations during favorable as well as unfavorable economic times. In good economic times, expenditures increase and organizational leaders are concerned that investments are properly allocated. In tough economic times, programs and processes that yield the best results are most likely to survive reorganization and restructuring efforts. Whether the organization is a large insurance company, a computer manufacturer, a federal or local government agency, or a non-governmental organization, a comprehensive evaluation process can help to pinpoint the areas in which to place available funding.

Characteristics of Organizations Using ROI

While the ROI Methodology is suitable for any organization, the organizations currently implementing ROI as part of their evaluation process share some characteristics, such as the following:

Size of the organization. Currently, organizations implementing ROI are typically large. Whether in the public or private sector, large organizations tend to deliver a variety of programs to a diverse target audience—usually throughout a vast geographical area. Organizations delivering a variety of programs usually have some programs they could do without, and it is important to ensure that they are offering the right programs, for the right reasons, at the right times, to the right people. Large organizations also have the budgets necessary to develop comprehensive evaluation approaches. However, ROI *should* be built into the accountability process in smaller organizations as well. Small organizations have even greater reason to conserve resources and ensure that they are getting the most out of their dollars. Using several cost-saving approaches described later, small organizations (and larger organizations with limited budgets) can implement ROI with credible results.

Size and visibility of the budget. Organizations implementing ROI usually allocate large budgets to programs such as those in the learning, performance improvement, and human resources functions. Some organizations allocate as much as $1 billion to these types of programs. The size of the budget has the attention of the senior management team. Regardless of how it is measured, whether as total budget, expenditure per employee, percentage of payroll, or percentage of revenue, a large budget brings appropriate focus to additional measurement and evaluation. Executives will demand increased accountability for large expenditures.

Focus on measurement. Typically, organizations implementing ROI focus on establishing a variety of measures throughout the organization. Organizations already using well-known processes such as the Balanced Scorecard, Six Sigma, and others are ideal candidates for the ROI Methodology because they already have measurement-focused environments.

Key drivers requiring additional accountability. The presence of the drivers discussed earlier brings additional focus to accountability. These drivers create the need to change current practices. In most situations, multiple drivers create interest in ROI accountability.

Level of change taking place. Organizations using ROI are usually undergoing significant change. As an organization adjusts to competitive pressures, it is transforming, restructuring, and reorganizing. Significant change often increases interest in bottomline issues, resulting in a need for greater accountability.

Symptoms that an Organization Is Ready for ROI

Several revealing symptoms indicate that an organization is ready to implement ROI. Many of these symptoms reflect the key drivers discussed earlier, which cause pressure to pursue ROI.

1. **Pressure from senior management to measure results.** This pressure can be a direct requirement to measure program effectiveness or a subtle expression of concern about the accountability of programs and processes.

2. **Extremely low investments in measurement and evaluation.** As indicated earlier, most organizations spend about 1 percent of their budget on measurement and evaluation processes. Investments significantly lower than this amount may indicate that there is little, if any, measurement or evaluation taking place, signaling the need for greater accountability. Expenditures in the 3–5 percent range indicate that learning and development and human resources functions are undergoing serious evaluation.

3. **Recent program disasters.** Every organization has experienced situations in which a major program was implemented without success. When there are multiple program failures, the function owning the programs often bears direct responsibility—or at least blame. These failures may prompt the implementation of measurement and evaluation processes to determine the impact

of programs, or more appropriately, to forecast ROI prior to implementation.

4. **A new director or leader in the function.** A new leader often serves as a catalyst for change and may initiate a review of previous programs' success rates. These individuals do not have the stigma of ownership or attachment to old programs and are willing to take an objective view. However, the desire to gain an immediate gauge of program effectiveness may lead to impatience if an evaluation process is not already in place.

5. **Managers' desire to build cutting-edge functions.** Some managers strive to build cutting-edge functions. In doing so, they may automatically build comprehensive measurement and evaluation processes into the overall strategy. These managers often set the pace for measurement and evaluation by highlighting the fact that they are serious about bringing accountability to their functions. These functions have formal guidelines around their measurement processes and build evaluation into program development. They often begin with thorough needs assessments to determine the best solutions, then monitor the progress of the programs and determine the business impact.

6. **Lack of management support.** In some cases, the image of a function suffers to the point that management no longer supports its efforts. While the unsatisfactory image may be caused by a number of factors, increased accountability often focuses on improving systems and processes, thereby shoring up the department's image.

Table 2 provides a self-check to determine your organization's candidacy for ROI implementation.

Table 2. ROI Readiness Self-Check

Is Your Organization A Candidate for ROI Implementation?

Check the most appropriate level of agreement for each statement:
1 = Strongly Disagree; 5 = Strongly Agree

	1	2	3	4	5
1. My organization is considered a large organization with a wide variety of programs.	☐	☐	☐	☐	☐
2. We have a large budget that attracts the interest of senior management.	☐	☐	☐	☐	☐
3. Our organization has a culture of measurement and is focused on establishing a variety of measures in all functions and departments.	☐	☐	☐	☐	☐
4. My organization is undergoing significant change.	☐	☐	☐	☐	☐
5. There is pressure from senior management to measure results of our programs.	☐	☐	☐	☐	☐
6. My function currently has a very low investment in measurement and evaluation.	☐	☐	☐	☐	☐
7. My organization has experienced more than one program disaster in the past.	☐	☐	☐	☐	☐
8. My department has a new leader.	☐	☐	☐	☐	☐
9. My team would like to be the leaders in our field.	☐	☐	☐	☐	☐
10. The image of our department is less than satisfactory.	☐	☐	☐	☐	☐
11. My clients are demanding that our processes show bottomline results.	☐	☐	☐	☐	☐
12. My function competes with other functions within our organization for resources.	☐	☐	☐	☐	☐
13. There is increased focus on linking our process to the strategic direction of the organization.	☐	☐	☐	☐	☐
14. My function is a key player in change initiatives currently taking place in the organization.	☐	☐	☐	☐	☐
15. Our overall budget is growing and we are required to prove the bottomline of value of our processes.	☐	☐	☐	☐	☐

Scoring

If you scored:

15–30	You are not yet a candidate for ROI.
31–45	You are not a strong candidate for ROI; however, it is time to start pursuing some type of measurement process.
46–60	You are a candidate for building skills to implement the ROI process. At this point there is no real pressure to show the ROI, which is the perfect opportunity to perfect the process within the organization.
61–75	You should already be implementing a comprehensive measurement and evaluation process, including ROI.

CHAPTER 2: THE EVALUATION PUZZLE

Developing a credible and comprehensive measurement and evaluation process is much like putting together a puzzle. The Evaluation Puzzle in Figure 1 represents all of the major elements.

The first piece of the puzzle is the *evaluation framework*. This framework defines the levels at which programs are evaluated and how data are captured at different times from different sources. The second piece of the puzzle is the *ROI process model*. An ROI model is critical in that it depicts systematic steps to ensure consistent application of the evaluation methodology. The third piece of the evaluation puzzle is *operating standards or guiding principles*. These standards build credibility into the process by supporting a systematic methodology and conservative approach to ROI evaluation. The standards and guiding principles also support consistency in the process. The fourth piece of the evaluation puzzle is *case application and practice*. Case studies show real-world applications of the process and provide support for implementation. The final piece of the puzzle, *implementation,* brings together the other four pieces to implement the ROI Methodology. Critical elements of implementation, which will be discussed later, ensure that the evaluation process is fully integrated into the organization; that the organization develops the appropriate skills, procedures, and guidelines; and that a comprehensive communication strategy is in place to ensure that the process is utilized to its fullest while maintaining credibility with key stakeholders.

Figure 1. Evaluation Puzzle

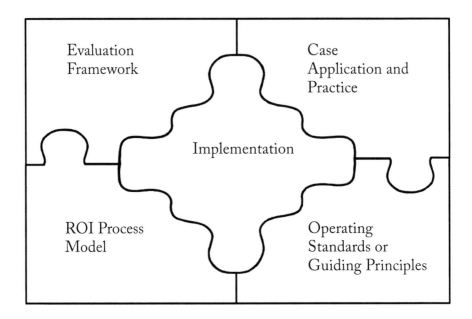

Together, these five pieces of the evaluation puzzle form a comprehensive measurement and evaluation system that contains a balanced set of measures, has credibility, and can be replicated from one group to another. The remainder of this book explains the various pieces of the evaluation puzzle, with a focus on the ROI model.

Evaluation Framework

The first piece of the evaluation puzzle is the evaluation framework. An important contribution to the field of training measurement and evaluation is the work of Donald Kirkpatrick. In the 1950s, Kirkpatrick developed what was originally referred to as four steps to evaluation, but is now known as the four levels of evaluation. Table 3 presents the four levels and their respective definitions.

Table 3. Kirkpatrick's Four-Level Evaluation Framework

Level	Brief Description
1 – Reaction	Measures participant reaction to the program
2 – Learning	Measures the extent to which participants change attitudes, improve knowledge, and/or increase skills
3 – Behavior	Measures the extent to which change in behavior occurs
4 – Results	Measures changes in business results

The first of Kirkpatrick's four levels is Reaction, a measure of participant reaction to the program. Level 2, Learning, is the measure of changes in participant attitudes, knowledge, or skills as a result of the program. Kirkpatrick defines Level 3, Behavior, as the measure of change in behavior on the job after attending the program. Kirkpatrick's fourth level, Results, measures changes in business results such as productivity, quality, costs, sales, turnover, and higher profits (Kirkpatrick 1994).

Kirkpatrick's work provides the initial framework for evaluating learning and performance improvement programs. However, the need to take evaluation a step further continues to intensify. Increasingly, executives require the learning, performance improvement, and human resources functions to show the value they bring to the organization in the same terms as other operational functions. The most common measure for value-added benefits in other operational functions is return on investment (Horngren 1982; Anthony and Reece 1983). As presented earlier, ROI is the comparison of earnings (net benefits) to investment (costs) (Kearsley 1982).

In order to address the need to show financial contribution to the organization while balancing the data with the additional measures, Jack Phillips expanded Kirkpatrick's four levels to add a fifth level, ROI (Phillips 1983), and redefined the levels to address specific measures taken and questions answered through the measurement process. In addition, he provided the process model and standards to support actual application of evaluation at each level. Table 4 illustrates Phillips' five-level evaluation framework.

Table 4. Phillips' Five-Level Evaluation Framework

Level	Measurement Focus	Key Questions Answered
1 Reaction and Planned Action	Measures participant satisfaction with the program or process and captures planned actions	Is the program or process relevant, important, useful, and helpful to the participant and the job environment?
2 Learning	Measures changes in knowledge, skills, and attitudes	Did participants increase or enhance knowledge, skills, or perceptions? Do they understand the information shared? Do they have the confidence to do what they need to do?
3 Application and Implementation	Measures changes in performance or action	Are participants applying the knowledge/skills/information? If yes, what is supporting them? If no, why not?
4 Business Impact	Measures changes in key business measures	How does the application improve output, quality, cost, time, and satisfaction? How do we know it was the program that caused this improvement?
5 ROI	Compares the program benefits to the costs	Do the monetary benefits of the program exceed the investment in the program?

The addition of Level 5 ROI takes into account the steps of the cost-benefit analysis process and the calculation of the ROI percentage. Where Kirkpatrick's fourth level stops at identifying the benefits of the program (Level 4, Results), Phillips' Level 5 converts the benefits to monetary value and compares those monetary benefits to the fully loaded costs of the program (Phillips 1996b), bringing into the framework new data not captured at Level 4. To ensure accuracy in calculating the return on investment, Phillips also includes a critical step—isolating the effects of the program (Phillips 1996a). Isolating the effects ensures an accurate accounting of the program's benefits. Some people insist that if it is not possible to use classic experimental design to isolate the effects of a program, this step will not be valid and should not be taken (Benson and Tran 2002). However, other appropriate techniques are available and will be discussed later in the book. Excluding this step entirely results in incorrect, invalid, and inappropriate business impact and ROI calculations.

Table 5 provides a comparison of Kirkpatrick's framework, Phillips' framework, and the cost-benefit analysis process. As shown in Table 5, both Kirkpatrick and Phillips address participant reaction as well as learning and application of skills, or behavior change. Level 4 (Impact/Results) is comparable to the identification of benefits in cost-benefit analysis; however, Phillips' framework is the only one of the three that addresses the issue of accounting for other influences. Level 5, ROI, includes the cost-benefit analysis steps to convert data to monetary value and to tabulate the fully loaded program costs. Kirkpatrick, Phillips, and cost-benefit analysis all consider the intangible benefits of implementing a program.

Table 5. Evaluation Frameworks Compared to Cost–Benefit Analysis

	Kirkpatrick's Four Levels	Phillips's Five Levels	CBA
Measure Participant Reaction	X	X	
Measure Learning	X	X	
Measure Application/Behavior	X	X	
Measure Impact/Results	X	X	X
Measure ROI		X	X
Isolate the Effects of the Program		X	
Determine Cost		X	X
Convert Benefits to Monetary Value		X	X
Identify Intangible Benefits	X	X	X

Although this distinction between the frameworks is important, it is necessary to understand that not all programs should be evaluated at all five levels. Perhaps the best explanation for this is that as the level of evaluation increases, so does its difficulty and expense. It takes time and resources to conduct a comprehensive ROI study, so it is not feasible to do it for every program. Table 6 suggests some targets for evaluating programs at different levels.

Table 6. Suggested Evaluation Targets

Evaluation Levels	Percent of Programs to Evaluate at Each Level
Level 1 Reaction	90 – 100%
Level 2 Learning	60 – 80%
Level 3 Application	30 – 50%
Level 4 Impact	10 – 20%
Level 5 ROI	5 – 10%

Some programs should be evaluated just for reaction, some just for learning, etc. Programs are selected for evaluation using criteria such as these:

- Expected program life cycle
- Importance of the program in meeting the organization's goals
- Cost of the program
- Visibility of the program
- Size of the target audience
- Extent of management interest

However, when evaluating at a higher level, it is important to evaluate at lower levels as well. A chain of impact occurs as participants react and plan action (Level 1) based on the knowledge, skills, and information acquired during the program (Level 2) which are then applied on the job (Level 3), resulting in improvement in business measures (Level 4). If measurements are not taken at each of these levels, it is difficult to:

- conclude that the results achieved are actually a result of the program;
- explain how results at the higher levels were achieved;
- provide relevant information to every stakeholder; and
- improve results based on an evidence-based breakdown in program implementation.

Because of these challenges, evaluation should be conducted at all levels when a Level 5 ROI evaluation is planned.

ROI Process Model

The second piece of the evaluation puzzle is the ROI process model. The ROI model shows the systematic steps to ensure that the evaluation methodology is implemented consistently. Replication of the evaluation process is imperative. A step-by-step model will ensure that this replication takes place following a systematic approach. Figure 2 shows the ROI Methodology process model. The model consists of four stages: Evaluation Planning, Data Collection, Data Analysis, and Reporting. The model will be explored in the next two chapters.

Figure 2. The ROI Process Model

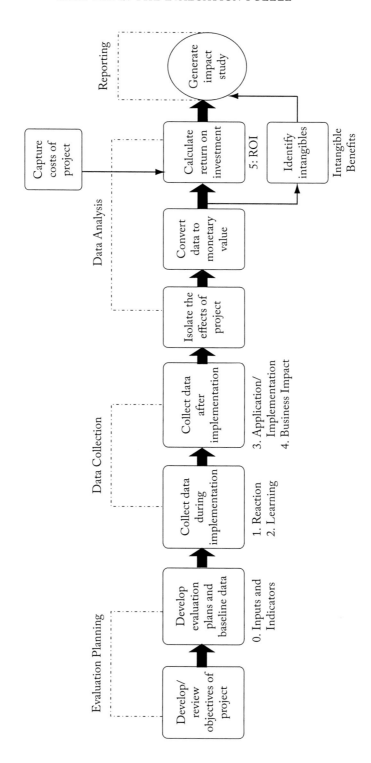

Operating Standards: Guiding Principles

Operating standards, the third piece of the evaluation puzzle, help to ensure that there is consistency in the evaluation process and that a conservative approach is taken. Standards or guiding principles keep the evaluation credible and support replication of the process. When implementing ROI, there are twelve guiding principles to use as operating standards.

1. Tell the Complete Story of Program Success

When a higher level of evaluation is conducted, data must be collected at lower levels. ROI is a critical measure, but it is only one of the measures necessary to explain the full impact of a program, so lower levels of data must be included in the analysis. The data at the lower levels also provide important information that can be helpful in making adjustments for future program implementation.

2. Conserve Resources for Higher-Level Evaluations

When an evaluation is planned for a higher level, the previous level of evaluation does not have to be comprehensive. Lower-level measures are critical in telling the complete story, and cannot be omitted. However, shortcuts can be taken to conserve resources. For example, when the client is interested in business impact, shortcuts can be taken at Levels 2 and 3.

3. Use the Most Credible Sources

When collecting and analyzing data, use only the most credible sources. Credibility is the most important factor in the measurement and evaluation process. Without it, the results are meaningless. Collecting data from the most credible source (often the participants) will enhance the perception of the quality and accuracy of data analysis and results.

4. Choose the Most Conservative Alternative

When analyzing data, select the most conservative alternative for calculations. This principle is at the heart of the evaluation process. A conservative approach lowers the ROI and helps to build the needed credibility with the target audience. It is always better to be conservative than to provide a generous estimate and overstate results.

5. Give Credit Where Credit is Due

At least one method must be used to isolate the effects of the solution. This step is imperative. Without some method to isolate the effects of the program, the evaluation results are considered inaccurate and overstated.

6. Make No Assumptions for Non-Respondents

If no improvement data are available for a population or from a specific source, it is assumed that little or no improvement has occurred. If participants do not provide data—if they are no longer a part of the organization or they perform a different function—assume that little or no improvement has occurred. It damages the credibility of the evaluation to make assumptions about improvements of which you cannot be sure. This ultraconservative approach further enhances the credibility of the results.

7. Adjust Estimates for Error

Estimates of improvements should be adjusted for the potential error of the estimate. This guideline contributes to the conservative approach of the process. Using estimates is very common in reporting financial and cost-benefit information. To enhance the credibility of estimated data used in ROI evaluation of learning and performance improvement programs, estimates are weighted with a level of confidence, adjusting the estimate for potential error.

8. Omit the Extremes

Extreme data items and unsupported claims should not be used in ROI calculations. Again, to maintain credibility of the results, steps should be taken to be conservative in the analysis. For example, if you have a list of numbers all ranging from 30 to 70 and only one 100, that 100 would be considered an outlier or extreme data item. Extreme data items can skew results both to the low side as well as the high side. In order to eliminate the influence of extreme data items, omit them from the analysis.

9. Report First-Year Benefits Only for Short-Term Programs

Only the first year of benefits (annual) should be used in the ROI analysis of short-term solutions. If benefits are not quickly realized for most learning and performance improvement programs, they are probably not worth the cost. Therefore, for short-term programs, consider only first-year benefits. For more extensive programs, where implementation spans a year or more, multiple-year benefits are captured.

10. Account for All Program Costs

Costs of the solution should be fully loaded for ROI analysis. All costs of the program are tabulated, beginning with the cost of the needs analysis and ending with the cost of the evaluation. As part of the conservative approach, the costs are loaded to reduce the ROI.

11. Report Intangible Benefits

Intangible measures are defined as measures that are purposely not converted to monetary values. While the ROI is the ultimate measure of program success, it is important to report the intangible benefits. Intangible benefits such as customer satisfaction, employee engagement, better teamwork, and innovation are important measures of program success. Sometimes the intangibles carry as much weight with senior executives as a program's financial benefits.

12. Communicate and Use Evaluation Data

The results from the ROI Methodology must be communicated to all key stakeholders. The purpose of evaluating programs using ROI Methodology is to report success, gain respect, influence decisions, and improve programs. If evaluation results are not reported and used, then evaluation becomes just another activity. Activity represents cost, and costs get cut. Just like your programs, ensure that your evaluation practice is positioned as an investment.

Table 7 summarizes these guiding principles. Collectively, these standards ensure that the evaluation approach is conservative and that the impact study can be replicated, making them a crucial part of the puzzle. They also ensure that the ROI for programs such as learning and development, performance improvement, and human resources can be compared to the ROI of operational processes and initiatives in the organization.

Table 7. Twelve Guiding Principles

Operating Standards / Guiding Principles

Guiding Principle	Meaning
1. When a higher level of evaluation is conducted, data must be collected at lower levels.	Tell the complete story of program success.
2. When an evaluation is planned for a higher level, the previous level of evaluation does not have to be comprehensive.	Conserve resources for the higher-level evaluations.
3. When collecting and analyzing data, use only the most credible sources.	Use the most credible sources.
4. When analyzing data, choose the most conservative alternative for calculations.	Choose the most conservative alternative.

5. At least one method must be used to isolate the effects of the solution.	Give credit where credit is due.
6. If no improvement data are available for a population or from a specific source, it is assumed that little or no improvement has occurred.	Make no assumptions for non-respondents.
7. Estimates of improvements should be adjusted for the potential error of the estimate.	Adjust estimates for error.
8. Extreme data items and unsupported claims should not be used in ROI calculations.	Omit the extremes.
9. Only the first year of benefits (annual) should be used in the ROI analysis for short-term solutions.	Report only first year benefits for short-term programs.
10. Costs of the solution should be fully loaded for ROI analysis.	Account for all program costs.
11. Intangible measures are defined as measures that are purposely not converted to monetary values.	Report intangible benefits.
12. The results from the ROI Methodology must be communicated to all key stakeholders.	Communicate and use your evaluation data.

Case Application and Practice

A critical piece of the evaluation puzzle is the development of case studies by the various functions to show success, to promote programs, or to justify new programs. Case studies from other organizations can also be used as benchmarks or examples of success. Case studies within similar industries indicate the status of ROI implementation in similar organizations—addressing similar issues and targeting similar concerns. Case studies from a global perspective provide evidence of success with the ROI Methodology in a variety of organizations and industries, supporting the need to pursue comprehensive measurement and evaluation. Case studies also provide support to practitioners, managers, and executives interested in learning about how to apply the ROI Methodology.

The use of case studies from other organizations is helpful in understanding the merits of ROI implementation and the success of specific programs. Studies developed by the implementing organization, however, are more powerful in displaying evidence of success using the ROI Methodology to evaluate internal programs. Table 8 provides a summary of examples of applications of ROI.

Table 8. Sample Case Studies

Measuring the ROI:	Key Impact Measures:	ROI
Performance Management (Restaurant Chain)	A variety of measures, such as productivity, quality, time, costs, turnover, and absenteeism	298%[1]
Process Improvement Team (Apple Computer)	Productivity and labor efficiency	182%[1]
Employee Retraining (Codelco)	Dispatch and power view indicators	115%[8]
Sexual Harassment Prevention (Health Care Chain)	Complaints, turnover, absenteeism, job satisfaction	1,052%[2]
Sales Training (Le Meridien Hotels)	Conference sales, conversion ratios, and rewards members	203%[8]
Diversity (Nextel Communications)	Retention, employee satisfaction	163%[6]
Retention Improvement (Financial Services)	Turnover, staffing levels, employee satisfaction	258%[3]
Electronic Documentation Tool (Caremark/CVS Pharmacy Operations)	Productivity, quality, materials cost	79.5%[8]

Stress Management Program (Electric Utility)	Medical costs, turnover, absenteeism	320%[2]
Executive Leadership Development (Financial)	Team projects, individual projects, retention	62%[2]
E-Learning (Petroleum)	Sales	206%[2]
Internal Graduate Degree Program (Federal Agency)	Retention, individual graduate projects	153%[4]
Executive Coaching (Nortel Networks)	Several measures, including productivity, quality, cost control, and product development time	788%[5]
Competency Development (Veterans Health Administration)	Time savings, work quality, faster response	159%[4]
First Level Leadership Development (Auto Rental Company)	Various measures – at least two per manager	105%[7]

[1] *In Action: Measuring Return on Investment*, Volume 3. Patricia Pulliam Phillips, Editor; Jack J. Phillips, Series Editor. Alexandria: ASTD, 2001.

[2] *The Human Resources Scorecard: Measuring the Return on Investment*. Jack Phillips, Ron D. Stone, Patricia Pulliam Phillips. Waltham, MA: Elsevier Butterworth-Heinemann, 2001.

[3] *In Action: Retaining Your Best Employees*. Patricia Pulliam Phillips, Editor; Jack J. Phillips, Series Editor. Alexandria: ASTD and the Society for Human Resource Management, 2002.

[4] *In Action: Measuring ROI in the Public Sector*. Patricia Pulliam Phillips, Editor. Alexandria: ASTD, 2002.

[5] *In Action: Coaching for Extraordinary Results*. Darelyn J. Mitch, Editor; Jack J. Phillips, Series Editor. Alexandria: ASTD, 2002.

[6] *In Action: Implementing Training Scorecards*. Lynn Schmidt, Editor; Jack J. Phillips, Series Editor. Alexandria: ASTD, 2003.

[7] *The Leadership Scorecard*. Jack J. Phillips and Lynn Schmidt, Waltham, MA: Elsevier Butterworth-Heinemann, 2004.

[8] *ROI in Action Casebook*. Patricia Pulliam Phillips and Jack J. Phillips. San Francisco: Pfeiffer, 2008.

Implementation

The final piece of the evaluation puzzle is implementation. The best tool, technique, or model will not be successful unless it is properly utilized and becomes a routine part of the function (Phillips 1997b). As with any change, the people affected by the implementation of a comprehensive measurement and evaluation process, including the staff and other stakeholders, will likely resist it. Part of that resistance will be based on realistic barriers. Part of it, however, will be based on misunderstandings and perceived problems. In both cases, the organization must work to overcome resistance by carefully and methodically implementing ROI evaluation using the following critical steps:

1. Assign responsibilities

2. Develop skills

3. Develop an implementation plan

4. Prepare or revise evaluation guidelines

5. Brief managers on the evaluation process

Assign Responsibilities

To ensure successful ROI implementation, assign responsibilities up front—before implementation begins. Who will lead the evaluation effort? Will evaluation be integrated into the function or will the evaluation leader report to the chief financial officer? Is it more appropriate to contract with a third-party evaluation provider and have only an internal coordinator? These questions and others must be considered when implementing any evaluation strategy.

Develop Skills

Another key step in successful implementation is the development of skills and capabilities. A complete understanding of each step in the evaluation process will simplify implementation, reducing the stress and frustration often associated with jumping from one process to another.

Develop an Implementation Plan

Planning for implementation will save time and money. By using a basic set of criteria to review existing programs as well as proposed new programs, the staff can develop an implementation plan. This plan will assist in determining which programs will be evaluated at which levels (by using the criteria discussed earlier) and how the necessary resources will be allocated.

Along with an implementation plan to select programs for different levels of evaluation, there should also be a project plan to help to manage the overall evaluation process. From a practical standpoint, this project plan serves to support the transition from the present situation to a desired future state. Table 9 provides a sample project plan.

Table 9. ROI Implementation Project Plan

PROJECT PLAN

	Oct	Nov	Dec	Jan	Feb	Mar	Apr	May	Jun	Jul	Aug	Sep
1. Review of Existing Programs, Processes, Reports, Data	▨	▨										
2. Develop Skills			▨									
3. Finalize Evaluation Planning Documents			▨	▨								
4. Collect Evaluation Data				▨	▨	▨	▨	▨	▨			
5. Analyze Evaluation Data									▨	▨	▨	
6. Develop Reports											▨	
7. Present Impact Study Results												▨
8. Develop Scorecard Framework									▨	▨	▨	
9. Develop Guidelines					▨	▨	▨	▨	▨	▨		
10. Brief Managers												

This particular project plan includes ten steps to implementing the ROI Methodology:

1. Review existing programs, processes, reports, and data. This step is essential to understanding past practices and how to incorporate the new methodology most effectively.

2. Develop skills. Developing the skills necessary to implement the ROI Methodology is essential for complete integration into the learning and development, performance improvement, or HR process.

3. Finalize evaluation planning documents. The planning documents necessary to implement the ROI Methodology are critical to ensure that every step of the process is taken and that key stakeholders agree with those steps.

4. Collect evaluation data. This step represents the data collection process.

5. Analyze evaluation data. This step represents the time necessary to analyze the data after collection.

6. Develop reports. As we will discuss in Chapter 4, developing a variety of reports helps to address specific audience needs. Of course, a complete impact study will be developed, but after the executive management understands the evaluation process, a brief summary (in some cases a single summary page will suffice) will be an appropriate method to communicate results.

7. Present impact study results. Different audiences need different information. In the initial implementation of the ROI Methodology, results should be presented in a formal setting to ensure clear communication of the process itself. Presentation of results to staff members may take place in a less formal setting such as a weekly staff meeting.

8. Develop scorecard framework. Sometimes it is important to show the results of an entire function. Unless ROI is calculated for all programs, it is not possible to show one ROI for the entire function. However, a scorecard allows the function or department to roll up data from all evaluations to show a macro-level view of success.

9. Develop guidelines. As the ROI Methodology is implemented and integrated into various functions and processes, guidelines are developed to ensure consistent and long-term implementation.

10. Brief managers. Management understanding of the evaluation process is critical. Managers who are not involved in a particular evaluation project might still be interested in the process. Manager briefings are a way to communicate not only the results of the evaluation but to communicate about the process in general. Each individual program evaluation will have individual project plans to detail the steps necessary to complete the project as well as to keep the evaluation project on track. Planning is the key to successful ROI implementation.

Prepare or Revise Evaluation Guidelines

Guidelines keep the implementation process on track. A clear set of guidelines helps to ensure that the process continues as designed in the event of changes in staff or management. They also establish the evaluation process as an integral part of the overall learning and performance improvement strategy.

Brief Managers on the Evaluation Process

Communicating to managers about the evaluation process will help to enlist their support during the implementation process. The unknown can often become a barrier, so if the organization makes the effort to explain each step, it is more likely that managers will understand and support the evaluation effort.

All five of the pieces of the evaluation puzzle are necessary to build a comprehensive measurement and evaluation process. The next two chapters describe the ROI Methodology step by step.

CHAPTER 3: THE ROI METHODOLOGY

An effective ROI Methodology must balance many issues, including feasibility, simplicity, credibility, and soundness, in part to satisfy the needs and requirements of three major target audiences. First, staff members who use the process must have a clear, straightforward approach. Otherwise, the process may appear confusing and complex, causing many staff members to assume that the ROI cannot be developed or that the process is too expensive for most applications. If staff members perceive the ROI Methodology as inconceivable, many will give up.

Second, the ROI Methodology must meet the unique requirements of the clients—those who request and approve programs. Clients need a process that will provide quantitative and qualitative results. They need a process that will develop a calculation similar to the ROI formula applied to other types of investment, and a process that reflects their frame of reference, background, and level of understanding. More importantly, they need a process with which they can identify—one that is sound, realistic, and practical enough to earn their confidence.

Finally, the process needs the support of researchers. The process must hold up under their scrutiny and close examination. Researchers want to use models, formulas, assumptions, and theories that are sound and based on commonly accepted practices. Also, they want a process that produces accurate values and consistent outcomes. They want a process that can be replicated reliably from one situation to another. If two different practitioners are evaluating a program, the process should result in the same measurements.

Criteria for an Effective ROI Process

An ROI process must adhere to certain criteria in order to meet the critical challenges of those who will be using it. The following criteria came out of working with learning and development, performance improvement, and human resources managers and specialists to develop comprehensive measurement and evaluation processes within their organizations.

Simple

An ROI process must be simple—devoid of complex formulas, lengthy equations, and complicated methodologies. Most ROI models do not meet these criteria. In an attempt to obtain statistical perfection, many ROI models and processes are too complex to understand and use. Consequently, they are not implemented. While there is merit in striving for statistical accuracy, if a model is so complicated that it cannot be used, the organization does not stand to benefit from it.

Economical

An ROI process must be economical and easily implemented. While the initial implementation of any new methodology can be costly, once that methodology is integrated into the organization and has become a routine part of the process, only minimal additional resources should be required to sustain its implementation.

Credible

The assumptions, methodology, and outcomes of the evaluation process must be credible. Logical, methodical steps earn the respect of practitioners, senior managers, and researchers. This requires not only a theoretically sound process, but a process that is practical in its approach as well.

Theoretically Sound

From a research perspective, the ROI Methodology must be theoretically sound and based on generally accepted practices. Unfortunately, this requirement can lead to an extensive, complicated process. Ideally, the process must strike a balance between maintaining a practical, sensible approach and ensuring a sound theoretical basis for the procedures. This is perhaps one of the greatest challenges to those who develop models for ROI measurement.

Accounts for Other Factors

An ROI process must account for other factors that influence output measures targeted by the program. This is one of the most often overlooked issues, but is necessary to build credibility and accuracy within the process. The ROI process should pinpoint the program's contribution while considering all other influences.

Appropriate

An ROI process should be appropriate for a variety of programs. Some models apply only to a small number of programs, such as those focused on productivity improvement. Ideally, the process must be applicable to every type of program, from career development and organizational development to major change initiatives. It is not practical for an organization to need a different evaluation process for every type of program.

Flexible

An ROI process must have the flexibility to be applied on a pre-program basis as well as a post-program basis. In some situations, an estimate of the ROI is required before developing the actual program. The process should be flexible enough to adjust to a range of potential time frames for calculating ROI.

Applicable

An ROI process must be applicable with both hard and soft data. Hard data are typically represented as output, quality, cost, and time. Soft data include job satisfaction, customer satisfaction, absenteeism, turnover, grievances, and complaints.

Considers All Costs

An ROI process must include all of the fully loaded costs associated with programs. These costs include: the initial needs assessment; development; delivery costs including facilitator, facility, and participant costs; and evaluation costs. Although the term ROI has been loosely used to express any of the benefits of a program, an acceptable ROI process includes all costs compared to monetary benefits. Omitting or understating program costs will overstate the ROI, and thus destroy its credibility.

Successful Track Record

Finally, an ROI process needs a successful track record with a variety of types of applications. In far too many situations, models that might look good but that are never applied successfully are created. An effective measurement and evaluation process should withstand the wear and tear of implementation and prove valuable to users. These criteria are essential; to be worthwhile for an organization, an ROI process should meet the vast majority, if not all, of these criteria. The bad news, however, is that most models do not. Table 10 provides a checklist that you can use to evaluate processes against the criteria.

Table 10. Criteria for a Credible ROI Process
How Does Your Measurement and Evaluation Process Compare?

Criteria	ROI Methodology	Balanced Scorecard	Economic Value Added	Other	Other
Simple	X				
Economical	X				
Credible	X				
Theoretically sound	X				
Accounts for other factors	X				
Appropriate with a variety of programs	X				
Applicable on pre-program and post-program basis	X				
Measures both hard and soft data	X				
Includes all fully loaded costs	X				
Successful track record	X				

The ROI Methodology

The ROI Methodology process model shown in Figure 2 (see page 33) generates five levels of results: reaction and planned action (Level 1); learning (Level 2); application and implementation (Level 3); business impact (Level 4); and ROI (Level 5). In addition, business impact measures that are not converted to money are reported as a sixth type of data—these are the intangibles.

As shown, the process also includes the critical step of isolating the effects of the program. This ROI Methodology, developed by Dr. Jack Phillips, provides a balanced approach to evaluating all types of programs and initiatives. It meets all of the criteria for an effective ROI process.

The process is divided into four stages. The first stage addresses *evaluation planning*. This critical step begins with the development of program objectives and comprehensive evaluation plans. The second stage represents the *data collection* process. Data are collected from different sources to develop a balanced set of measures. The third stage of the process is *data analysis*. At this stage, the practitioners isolate the program from other influences, convert data to monetary value, tabulate program costs, and calculate the ROI. It is also at this stage that the intangible benefits, those benefits not converted to monetary value, are identified. The final stage of the process is *reporting*. The last step in this comprehensive process, reporting results, is one of the most critical stages and will be explored in detail in the next chapter.

Evaluation Planning

The first stage of the ROI Methodology, evaluation planning, is one of the most critical. Thorough planning ensures that the evaluation addresses the appropriate objectives and utilizes the appropriate data collection instruments, and that the client agrees on data analysis procedures. The evaluation planning stage includes two steps: developing program objectives and developing the evaluation plan.

Develop Program Objectives

Before ROI evaluation begins, the program objectives must be developed. The objectives form the basis for determining the depth of the evaluation, meaning that they determine what level of evaluation will take place. Program objectives range from participant reaction to the actual ROI calculation. Program objectives link directly to the results of the front-end analysis, or needs assessment. Figure 3 demonstrates the alignment between needs, objectives, and evaluation. As shown, the needs assessment process begins with identifying the potential payoff or opportunity for an organization or function (Level 5 Needs). With this in mind, the business needs are then identified (Level 4 Needs). A thorough needs analysis follows to identify the performance needs (Level 3 Needs) that, if addressed, will help address the business needs. The knowledge, skills, and information needed to achieve the desired performance are identified (Level 2 Needs), taking into consideration the participants' preferences for learning (Level 1 Needs). For each of these levels of need, it is necessary to develop objectives and then to link those objectives to levels of evaluation. This will ensure that the right questions are asked during the evaluation process. This process of alignment ensures that programs are positioned for success and that the evaluation process considers the appropriate measures.

Figure 3. Business Alignment Model

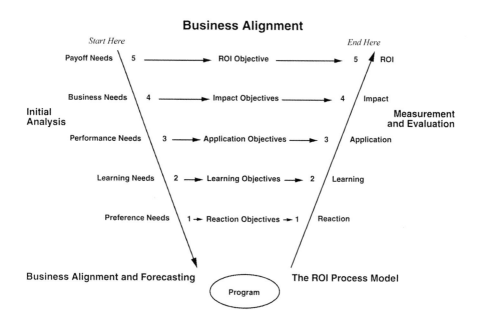

Table 11 shows an example of how the alignment process comes together for a particular program. To check your understanding of the five-level framework, complete the exercise on page 56.

Table 11. Example of Alignment

Sample Linkage Between Needs, Objectives, and Evaluation				
Level	Needs	Objectives	Evaluation	Level
5	$1.6 million costs due to falsely rejected syringes	25% ROI	• Program costs compared to monetary benefits of program • Monetary benefit determined by cost savings of reduced number of false rejects	5
4	False rejects are a problem; false rejects defined as syringes rejected when they are actually usable	• Reduce the number of false rejects by 10% within six months	• Monitor false rejects for six months • Participant estimates used for isolation	4
3	Inspectors are incorrectly identifying syringes as unacceptable	• Follow the five-step process during 100% of inspections • Utilize job aid as needed • Identify barriers to following the five-step process	• Follow-up questionnaire to participants to check frequency of skill application and barriers three months after the training • Unscheduled audits over six months	3
2	Deficiency in skills to recognize unacceptable syringes	• Demonstrate the five-step process and ability to follow job aid • Know the difference between acceptable and unacceptable syringes • Describe the consequences of incorrectly categorizing syringes	• Demonstrate ability to identify acceptable and unacceptable syringes • Indicate knowledge and understanding by completing learning assessment	2

Level	Needs	Objectives	Evaluation	Level
1	One-day workshop and introduction to new job aid	• Program receives favorable rating of 4 out of 5 on the following: 　◦ Relevance of workshop content and job aid 　◦ Importance of following the five-step inspection process 　◦ Intent to use job aid during inspections 　◦ Other measures important to design and delivery of content	• Reaction questionnaire administered at the end of the workshop	1

Exercise: Matching Objectives with Levels of Evaluation

Instructions: For each objective listed below, indicate the level of evaluation at which the objective is aimed.

Level 1 – Reaction and Planned Action
Level 2 – Learning
Level 3 – Application and Implementation
Level 4 – Business Impact
Level 5 – Return on Investment

Objective	Evaluation Level
1. Decrease error rates on reports by 20% within three months of the program	
2. Increase the use of disciplinary discussion skills in 90% of situations where work habits are unacceptable	
3. Achieve a post-test score increase of 30% over pre-test	
4. Within six weeks of completing the course, initiate at least three cost reduction projects as defined in the action plan	
5. Decrease the amount of time required to complete a project within three months of learning the software	
6. Achieve a 2:1 benefit-to-cost ratio one year after program implementation	
7. Receive an instructor rating from participants of at least 4.5 out of 5	
8. Increase the external customer satisfaction index by 25% in three months	
9. Handle customer complaints with the five-step process in 95% of complaint situations	
10. At least 50% of participants use all customer interaction skills with every customer	

Answers:

(1) L – 4; (2) L-3; (3) L-2; (4) L-3; (5) L-4; (6) L-5; (7) L-1; (8) L-4; (9) L-3; (10) L-3

Develop Evaluation Plan

After defining program objectives, the next step is to develop the evaluation plan. This plan is critical to ensure that each step of the evaluation process is addressed appropriately. As shown in Tables 12 and 13, the actual evaluation planning documents address each step of the process. The steps in the planning process include developing both a detailed data collection plan and a plan to analyze the data. The data collection plan should include broad program objectives. For planning purposes, only broad objectives are necessary. Next, the practitioner defines the specific measures that define the broader objectives. Determining how to evaluate each objective up front will save time and eliminate confusion later. The next steps include determining how to collect the data and from what sources to obtain them. Practitioners also determine the timing of the data collection during the initial planning stage, as well as who will be responsible for gathering the data items from the various sources.

After developing the data collection plan, Level 4 data items are copied to the ROI analysis plan. In this phase of the planning process, practitioners decide on the methods for isolating the effects of the program and converting data to monetary value. Program costs are identified, as are the Level 4 business measures that will not be converted to monetary value—the intangible benefits. Other potential influences that may affect the identified business measures are also noted during this phase. Finally, the target audiences for the final results are identified.

Table 12. Data Collection Plan

Data Collection Plan

Program: _____ Responsibility: _____ Date: _____

	Broad Program Objective(s)	Measures	Data Collection Method/Instruments	Data Sources	Timing	Responsibilities
L E V E L **1**	Reaction and Planned Action					
2	Learning and Confidence					
3	Application and Implementation					
4	Business Impact					
5	ROI					

Comments: _____

Table 13. ROI Analysis Plan

ROI Analysis Plan

Program: _____   Responsibility: _____   Date: _____

Data Items (Usually Level 4)	Methods for Isolating the Effects of the Program/Process	Methods of Converting Data to Monetary Values	Cost Categories	Intangible Benefits	Communication Targets for Final Report	Other Influences/ Issues During Application	Comments

Planning the evaluation is critical. Although much time and effort is put into this process, planning has many advantages:

- Planning provides a road map to complete the evaluation process.

- Agreeing up front with the client how the evaluation will take place will save frustration (for both parties) during the process.

- Presenting the plan to the program staff or project team, including program facilitators, will communicate expectations of program success and the process by which success will be measured. This step reinforces to the staff that the evaluation is a process-improvement tool, rather than an individual performance evaluation.

- Communicating the evaluation plan to program participants will reaffirm the importance of the program. It will also prepare participants to provide appropriate data at the appropriate time. This not only helps to ensure that credible data are received, but will also help to increase response rates during post-program follow-up.

Data Collection

The second stage of the ROI Methodology is data collection. Data are collected at two points—during program implementation and post-program implementation. Data are collected during the program to measure participants' reactions and to determine their planned actions. In addition, learning is measured to determine the extent to which participants acquired the knowledge, skills, and information necessary to improve performance. These measures help to ensure that adjustments are made as needed to keep the program on track. They also provide evaluators and program owners with an initial indication of a program's potential success. For example, if participants indicate that the content is relevant to their jobs and they appear to acquire the requisite knowledge, program owners can feel somewhat confident that participants will apply what they learned. If, however, participants indicate that the content is relevant to their jobs but all learning assessments show that they do not "get it," then the program owner needs to consider a follow-up mechanism to support participants' acquisition of knowledge.

Data are also collected on a post-program basis. Following the program, practitioners gather information regarding the application of skills and knowledge as well as the impact that the program has had on the organization. These data are collected sometime after the knowledge, skills, and information have begun to be applied routinely.

Both hard data and soft data are collected using a variety of methods such as the following:

- Attitudinal surveys
- Detailed questionnaires
- On-the-job observation
- Tests and assessments
- Interviews
- Focus groups
- Action plans
- Performance contracts
- Performance records

An important challenge in data collection is selecting the method or methods appropriate for the setting and the specific program, within the given time and budget constraints. Table 14 lists considerations for selecting data collection methods.

Table 14. Considerations When Selecting Data Collection Methods

When selecting data collection methods, consider the following:

- Type of data
  - Level of Evaluation
  - Quantitative versus Qualitative
  - Financial versus Intangible
- Time
  - Participant time required to provide data
  - Supervisor time required to provide data
- Costs
- Accuracy
  - Validity
  - Reliability
- Utility of Capturing Additional Data
- Organization Culture / Philosophy

Data Analysis

Data analysis is the third stage of the ROI Methodology. At this stage, results of the program begin to become clear. By isolating the effects of the program, results are more accurate—there is minimal question as to how much of the results can actually be attributed to the program. Data conversion takes place so that program benefits can be converted to monetary value. The costs are tabulated and the ROI calculation is developed in this stage. Finally, the intangible benefits are identified. Each of these steps is presented in greater detail below.

Isolate the Effects of the Program

An often-overlooked issue in evaluating programs and projects is the process of isolating the effects of the program. There are several specific strategies that determine the amount of performance improvement directly related to the program. Isolating the effects is essential because many factors will influence performance data after the implementation of a program. The specific strategies in this step will pinpoint the amount of improvement directly related to the program. The result is increased accuracy and credibility of the ROI Methodology results. The following are some commonly used strategies to address this important issue:

- A pilot group of participants in a program is compared with a control group not participating in the program to isolate program impact.

- Trend lines are used to project the values of specific output, and projections are compared with the actual data after the program.

- A forecasting model uses mathematical relationships between input and output variables to project output measures influenced by the program under evaluation.

- Participants estimate the amount of improvement that is related to the program.

- Supervisors and managers estimate the impact of the program on the output measures.

- External studies provide input about the impact of the program.

- Independent experts provide estimates of the impact of the program on the performance variable.

- When feasible, other influencing factors are identified and their impact is estimated or calculated, leaving the remaining unexplained improvement attributable to the program.

- Customers provide input about the extent to which the program has influenced their decisions to use a product or service.

Collectively, these strategies provide a comprehensive set of tools to address the important and critical issue of isolating the effects of programs and processes.

Convert Data to Monetary Values

To calculate the ROI, practitioners convert business impact data to monetary values and compare those values to program costs. This requires that a value be placed on each unit of data connected with the programs. The list below shows most of the key strategies used to convert data to monetary values. The specific strategy selected depends on the type of data and the situation:

- *Output data*, such as additional sales, are converted to profit contribution (or cost savings) and reported as a standard value.

- The cost of a *quality measure*, such as a customer complaint, is calculated and reported as a standard value.

- Employee *time saved* is converted to wages and benefits, a standard value.

- *Historical costs* of preventing a measure, such as a lost-time accident, are used when available.

- *Internal and external experts* estimate the value of a measure, such as an employee complaint.

- *External databases* contain the approximate value or cost of a data item, such as employee turnover.

- The measure is *linked to other measures* for which the costs are easily developed (e.g., employee satisfaction linked to turnover).

- *Participants estimate* the cost or value of the data item, such as work-group conflict.

- *Supervisors or managers estimate* costs or values, when they are willing and able, providing an estimate (e.g., an unscheduled absence).

- The *program staff estimates* the value of a data item, such as a sexual harassment complaint.

Converting data to monetary values is critical to determining the monetary benefits from programs. The process is challenging, particularly with soft data, but can be accomplished methodically using one or more of these strategies.

Capture Program Costs

The next step in the data analysis stage is capturing the costs of the program. Tabulating the costs involves monitoring or developing all of the costs related to the program. Costs related to programs include the following:

- Assessment costs

- Development costs

- Program materials

- Instructor/facilitator costs

- Facilities costs

- Travel/lodging/meals

- Participant salaries and benefits

- Administrative/overhead costs

- Evaluation costs

A fully loaded cost profile is recommended when tabulating all direct and indirect costs. Table 15 provides a sample cost summary detailing the fully loaded costs necessary to maintain a conservative

ROI calculation. Here is a general rule of thumb when it comes to calculating program costs:

When in doubt, leave it in.

By accounting for the full cost of a program, not only do you demonstrate a high level of accountability, but you ensure that the ROI is credible.

Table 15. Fully Loaded Cost Profile

FULLY LOADED COST PROFILE

Analysis Costs

Salaries and employee benefits
  (No. of people x average salary x employee
  benefits factor x hours on project)   _____

Meals, travel, and incidental expenses   _____

Office supplies and expenses   _____

Printing and reproduction   _____

Outside services   _____

Equipment expenses   _____

Registration fees   _____

General overhead allocation   _____

Other miscellaneous expenses   _____

A. Total Analysis Costs   _____

Development Costs

Salaries and employee benefits
  (No. of people x average salary x employee
  benefits factor x hours on project)   _____

Meals, travel, and incidental expenses   _____

Office supplies and expenses   _____

Program materials and supplies   _____

Videotape _____

CDs/DVDs _____

Artwork _____

Manuals and materials _____

Other _____

Printing and reproduction _____

Outside services _____

Equipment expenses _____

General overhead allocation _____

Other miscellaneous expenses _____

B. Total Development Costs _____

<u>Delivery Costs</u>

Participant costs _____

Salaries and employee benefits
(No. of participants x average salary x employee
benefits factor x time involved in the project) _____

Instructor costs _____

Salaries and benefits _____

Meals, travel, and incidental expenses _____

Outside services _____

Meals, travel, and accommodations
(No. of participants x average daily expenses
x days involved in the project) _____

Program materials and supplies _____

Participant replacement costs (if applicable) _____

Lost production (explain basis) _____

Facility costs _____

Facilities rental _____

Facilities expenses allocation _____

Equipment expenses _____

General overhead allocation _____

Other miscellaneous expenses _____

C. Total Delivery Costs _____

Evaluation Costs

Salaries and employee benefits
  (No. of people x average salary x employee
  benefits factor x hours on project)   _____

Meals, travel, and incidental expenses   _____

Participant cost   _____

Office supplies and expenses   _____

Printing and reproduction   _____

Outside services   _____

Equipment expenses   _____

General overhead allocation   _____

Other miscellaneous expenses   _____

D. Total Evaluation Costs   _____

Total Program Costs (A + B + C + D)   _____

Calculate the Return on Investment

As previously discussed, the return on investment is calculated by comparing the monetary benefits of a program to the costs. The benefit-cost ratio is the monetary benefits of the program divided by the costs. In formula form it is this:

$$BCR = \frac{\textbf{Program Benefits}}{\textbf{Program Costs}}$$

The return on investment uses the *net* benefits divided by costs. The net benefits are program benefits minus the costs. In formula form, ROI becomes:

$$ROI = \frac{\textbf{Net Program Benefits}}{\textbf{Program Costs}} \times 100$$

This is the same basic formula commonly used to evaluate other investments where ROI is traditionally reported as earnings divided by investment.

The BCR and ROI present the same general information but with slightly different perspectives. For example, say an effective meeting-skills program produced savings of $581,000, with a cost of $229,000. This would be the benefit-cost ratio:

$$\text{BCR} = \frac{\$581{,}000}{\$229{,}000} = 2.54 \text{ (or } 2.54{:}1)$$

As this calculation shows, every $1 invested in the program returned $2.54 in monetary benefits. However, to calculate ROI in this example, net benefits are $581,000 - $229,000 = $352,000. Thus, the ROI is this:

$$\text{ROI\%} = \frac{\$352{,}000}{\$229{,}000} \times 100 = 154\%$$

This means each $1 invested in the program returns approximately $1.54 in *net* benefits, after costs are covered. The benefits are usually expressed as annual benefits for short-term programs, representing the amount saved or gained for a complete year after the program has been implemented. Although the benefits may continue after the first year, the impact usually diminishes and is therefore omitted from calculations in short-term situations. For long-term projects, the benefits are spread over several years.

Identify Intangible Measures

In addition to tangible monetary benefits, most programs derive intangible non-monetary benefits. During data analysis, practitioners make every attempt to convert all data to monetary values. For example, hard data—such as output, quality, and time—are generally always converted to monetary values. Practitioners must also attempt to convert soft data. However, if the conversion process is too subjective or inaccurate and the resulting values lose credibility in the process, these data are labeled as intangible benefits and an appropriate explanation is provided. For some programs, intangible non-monetary benefits have extreme value, often commanding as much attention and influence as the hard data items (Moseley and Larson 1994). Intangible benefits include such items as the following:

- Improved public image

- Increased job satisfaction

- Increased organizational commitment

- Enhanced technology leadership

- Reduced stress

- Improved teamwork

- Improved customer service

This is not to say that these measures cannot be converted to money; rather, these are measures that typically do not need to be converted to money as they stand on their own quite well. In addition, to convert some measures to monetary values requires more resources than the entire evaluation, and the results are sometimes still not perceived as credible. So, here is a general rule of thumb when it comes to data conversion:

When in doubt, leave it out.

It is better to have a lower ROI with strong intangibles than to inflate the ROI by spending more on analysis and risking credibility.

Figure 4 provides a four-part test to determine whether or not you should convert a measure to money.

Figure 4. To Convert or Not To Convert

When trying to decide whether to convert a measure to money or to report it as an intangible benefit, ask yourself the following:

To Convert or Not To Convert

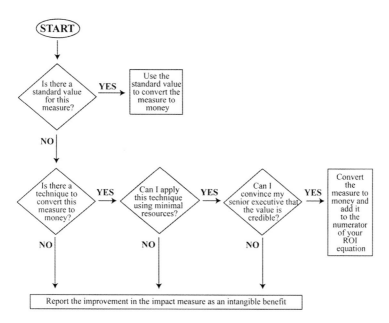

By following the steps in the ROI Methodology, six types of data evolve. Together, these data generate the chain of impact, as shown in Figure 5. This chain of impact occurs when participants are engaged in a program; when they react to the program; when they acquire the requisite knowledge, skill, and information; and when they apply them to the job or project. As a consequence of their application, key business measures improve. We know that this improvement is due to the program because the effects of the program are isolated from other influences. Impact measures are then converted to money and compared to the cost to generate the ROI. In addition, intangible benefits are reported. These six types of data tell the complete story of program success.

Figure 5. Chain of Impact

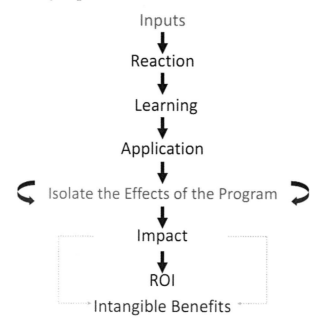

Reporting

The final stage in the ROI Methodology addresses the communication of results. This critical step includes several issues that are often neglected in the evaluation process. The communication process is often just as important as the evaluation itself, and what information is reported and how the information is reported are important concerns.

There are five key reasons why communicating results effectively is so important.

1. Measurement and evaluation mean nothing without communication. When an organization communicates the findings of a measurement and evaluation process to the appropriate audience at the appropriate time and in an effective manner, it creates a full loop from the program results to necessary actions based on those results.

2. Communicating results is necessary to make improvements. During program evaluation, information is collected at different points in time. Providing feedback to the various groups each step along the way will allow for adjustments and provide opportunities for improvement. Even after the program is complete, communication is necessary to make sure that the target audience understands the results achieved and how the results can enhance future programs as well as the current program. Communication is the key to making these important adjustments at all phases of the program.

3. Communication is necessary to show accountability in programs. Presenting results that encompass all six types of data will provide evidence of a program's contribution to the organization, but can also be quite confusing. Different target audiences need different levels of explanation around results.

4. Communication is a sensitive issue and can be a source of great benefit or a cause of major problems. Because program results can be closely linked to political issues in an organization, communication can upset some individuals while pleasing others. If certain individuals do not receive the information or it is delivered inconsistently from one group to another, problems can quickly surface.

5. A variety of target audiences need different information. Given that there are so many potential target audiences to deliver communication about program success to, it is important that the communication be tailored directly to their needs. Planning and effort are necessary to make sure that the audience receives all of the information it needs in the proper format and at the proper time. The scope, size, media, and even the actual information of different types and different levels may vary significantly from one group to another, making the target audience the key to determining the appropriate communication process. Communicating results effectively is essential to the success of the ROI Methodology. The next chapter outlines the necessary components of this crucial phase and discusses them in detail.

CHAPTER 4: COMMUNICATION OF RESULTS

Communicating results is the last step in the ROI Methodology. It is an important issue and one that deserves some attention. Communicating the results of a comprehensive measurement and evaluation process should be systematic and well-planned. Figure 6 provides a model of the six components necessary to ensure effective communication.

Figure 6. Communication Process Model

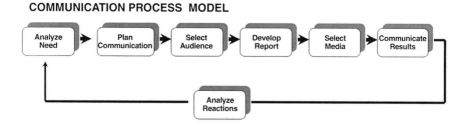

COMMUNICATION PROCESS MODEL

Analyze Need

The first step in the communication model is to analyze the need for the communication.

There are many reasons why it is important to communicate the results of a program:

- To secure approval for programs
- To gain support for the various functions

- To obtain commitment from participants in programs

- To build credibility for programs

- To reinforce the processes necessary to implement programs

- To explain the various issues around particular programs

- To demonstrate the importance of measuring results

- To market new and existing programs

- To satisfy clients' concerns regarding investments in various programs

There are numerous other reasons why communicating the results of program evaluation is important. Each individual organization should review the specific reasons and tailor its communication strategy around its needs.

Plan the Communication

Just as planning the evaluation process is important, so is planning the communication process. Thorough planning will ensure that the communication addresses both client concerns and issues important to the program staff and the general audience. Three issues are important in planning the communication of results:

1. Communication Guidelines

2. Communication around Specific Programs

3. Communicating the ROI Impact Study

Communication Guidelines

When examining the complete program or project implementation process, there should be guidelines for how the results will be communicated. These issues range from providing feedback during program implementation to communicating the ROI from an impact study. Seven areas should be considered in developing communication:

1. **What will actually be communicated?**

   It is important to detail the types of information communicated throughout the program.

2. **When will the data be communicated?**

   As with most projects and processes, timing is critical in communicating results.

3. **How will the information be communicated?**

   This shows preferences toward particular types of communication media. For example, some organizations prefer to have written documents, while others prefer face-to-face meetings, and still others prefer electronic forms of communication.

4. **Where will the communication take place**

   For some audiences, it may be more appropriate to present data in a formal on-site meeting; for others, it may be more appropriate to present data at an off-site, less formal location. The location is important in terms of convenience and perception.

5. **Who will communicate the results?**

   Who the messenger will be is another important issue to consider. Is it most appropriate for the program manager to present results? An independent third party? In any event, it is critical to consider the question when developing the overall communication strategy.

6. **Who should receive the information?**

    Identifying the target audience is another crucial issue. The client should receive a detailed report or, at the least, a presentation that reflects the detailed information. The general population of the organization should receive highlights. Ensuring that the appropriate audience receives the appropriate information is critical in achieving the desired response.

7. **What actions are required or desired as a result of the communication?**

    The final consideration in developing the communication plan is determining what actions are required or desired as a result of the communication. A communication to the program staff may explain changes that need to be made to the program; a communication to senior executives may be a call for a change in priorities. Clearly stating the desired outcomes of the communication is an important part of developing the overall strategy.

Communication around Specific Programs

When a specific program has been approved and the evaluation process is being planned, the communication plan should be developed along with the other evaluation planning documents. This plan details how specific information will be developed and communicated to various groups and what actions will be expected. In addition, this plan details how the overall results will be communicated, the time frames for communication, and the appropriate groups to receive information.

Communicating the ROI Impact Study

The final issue regarding communication planning is the communication of the final ROI impact study. The presentation of this study occurs at the completion of the evaluation process, when the results of all levels of evaluation have been analyzed. Different audiences need different levels of detail. For instance, the evaluation team and program staff will generally always receive a copy of the complete report. This complete report details the need for and objectives of the program, as well as the methodology used and the results of the evaluation. The data collection instruments and raw data appear in an appendix.

When the evaluation process becomes routine, and senior and executive management are familiar with the process and the reporting format, a one-page summary of results can be used. This one-page report, as shown in Table 16, provides the essential details and program results in a brief, bottomline format. A word of caution: while this report provides a quick look at the results, it is not advisable to begin reporting results in this format until the evaluation process is well-supported within an organization and by senior and executive management. Also, as will be explained later, a formal presentation should be made to senior staff at least once to ensure that they understand the process and perceive the results as credible.

Table 16. Sample Micro-Level Scorecard

Large Telecommunications Company

Program Title: Diversity
Target Group: Managers and Employees
Solution: All-Inclusive Workforce Program (AIW)

RESULTS

Level 1: Reaction and Planned Action	Level 2: Learning and Confidence	Level 3: Application and Implementation	Level 4: Impact	Level 5: ROI	Intangible Benefits
Composite Rating: 4.39 out of 5 (for six items)	Averaged 4.28 out of 5 (for learning on six objectives)	Managers: Supports AIW (87%) Addresses Problems (81%) Encourages Staff (78%)	Attrition Rate Improvement = 9.77%	BCR: 2.6 ROI: 163%	Employee Satisfaction Communication Cooperation Diversity Mix Teamwork
		Employees: Supports AIW (65%) Identifies Differences (63%) Encourages Staff (60%)			
		91% of Managers successfully completed action plans			

Technique to Isolate Effects of Program: Managers' estimates, adjusted for error
Technique to Convert Data to Monetary Value: Standard cost item ($89,000 per turnover)
Fully Loaded Program Costs: $1,216,836

Communication to other audiences may come in the form of general interest overviews, general interest articles, and marketing materials. Some of these will be discussed in more detail later. Table 18 is a sample communication plan. As shown, a complete report is provided for the client, staff, and project team. A much briefer report is provided for senior management. A general report is provided to participants. This step not only provides participants with program results, but also builds the credibility of the ROI Methodology. Participants spend time completing questionnaires and participating in focus groups and interviews during the evaluation process. As part of their participation, they should be provided with the results.

A general interest article can be printed in a company publication. This type of article keeps accountability for the learning and development, performance improvement, and/or human resources functions in front of the employees at large. Finally, ROI results are published in marketing brochures to recruit participants for future programs. The key is to plan the communication of the final impact study with the various report types and audiences in mind.

Table 17. Communication Plan

COMMUNICATION PLAN

Impact Study Report	Target Audience	Distribution Method
Complete report (100 pages)	Client team Staff Project team	Special meeting
Executive summary (8 pages)	Senior management	Routine meeting
General interest overview and summary (10 pages)	Participants	Mail with letter
General interest article (1 page)	All employees	Company newsletter
Brochure highlighting project objectives and specific results	Team leaders Other clients	Marketing materials

Select the Audience

To the greatest extent possible, the target audience for any communication should be identified in advance. Understanding audience needs and issues will ensure that the appropriate data from the evaluation process are communicated and that the desired results of the communication are achieved.

Along with understanding client needs and issues, there should also be a clear understanding of audience bias. While many audience members will quickly support the program results, others will be skeptical or even resentful. Understanding and expecting these biases will assist in ensuring that the communication process mitigates any preconceived biases. Some key questions to ask when assessing the audience are the following:

- Are they interested in the program?

- Do they want to receive the information?

- Has someone already made a commitment to them regarding communication?

- Is the timing right for this audience?

- Are they familiar with the program?

- How do they prefer to have results communicated?

- Are they likely to find the results threatening?

- Which medium will be most convincing to them?

Develop the Report

The next step in the communication process is to develop the final product—the comprehensive ROI evaluation impact-study report. This report presents the complete results of the ROI Methodology. As mentioned previously, the impact-study report provides details of the evaluation along with supporting documents and summary results. A basic report is usually divided into three sections: background information, results, and conclusions and recommendations.

Background Information

Background information gives an overview of the need for the program as well as a full description of it, if applicable. The description of the program includes program objectives as well as information on content, duration, course materials, facilitators, location, and other specific items.

In this initial section, the evaluation process is described in detail as well. The description is detailed enough to ensure that the audience will understand both the process and that the evaluation process can be replicated based on the information in the report. Along with information on the process, the data collection and data analysis strategies are detailed, including descriptions of the instruments used, the timing of the data collection, the sources of the data, isolation and data conversion techniques used, and cost categories considered.

Results

The next section presents the results of the evaluation. Each type of data generated by the ROI Methodology is reported, beginning with Level 0 (Inputs and Indicators), representing the program activity, then on to results at Level 1 (Reaction), and ending with intangible benefits. This balanced set of measures is reported so that the entire story is told. While ROI is a critical measure in the reporting process, it is only one of six measures of results. By presenting the results in order, the audience can better understand the full impact of the program, not just on the bottomline, but on the participants, processes, and the organization as a whole.

Conclusions and Recommendations

This section of the impact-study report presents the conclusions and brief explanations of how each conclusion came about. The section also includes a list of recommendations for changes to the program with brief explanations. It is important that the conclusions and recommendations be consistent with one another and with the findings described in the previous section.

Table 18 provides a sample table of contents from an ROI impact study, representing these three major sections. A complete impact study can vary in length from 20 to 30 pages for a small project up to 200 or more pages for a comprehensive evaluation. Remember that not all audiences need this detailed information. The key issue is to analyze the target audiences and develop reports that meet their needs.

Table 18. ROI Study Outline

Sample Table of Contents for an ROI Impact Study

Table of Contents
List of Tables
List of Figures
List of Exhibits

Part I The Challenge and the Approach

Section 1:   Introduction
Section 2:   The Program
Section 3:   Model for Impact Study
Section 4:   Data Collection Strategy
Section 5:   Data Analysis Strategy

Part II The Results

Section 6:   Inputs and Indicators
Section 7:   Reaction and Planned Action
Section 8:   Learning
Section 9:   Application and Implementation
         — Enablers to Application
         — Barriers to Application
Section 10: Business Impact
Section 11: ROI and Its Meaning
         — Monetary Benefits
         — Program Costs
         — ROI Calculation
Section 12: Intangible Benefits

Part III Recommendations

Section 13: Conclusions and Recommendations
Section 14: Suggestions for Improvement

Part IV Appendix

Select the Medium

There are many options available for communicating results. In addition to the actual report, the most frequently used media are management meetings, interim and progress reports, organization publications, and case studies.

Management Meetings

Management meetings are fertile ground for the communication of program results. All organizations have a variety of meetings and, in the proper context, program results can be an important part of each kind of meeting. Management meetings include staff meetings, supervisory meetings, panel discussions, and management association meetings.

Interim and Progress Reports

Interim and progress reports are brief reports mailed or emailed to the appropriate target audiences. A progress report can be something as simple as a "flash report" that appears when employees log on to email. Employees have the option to read it when they log on initially or to save it for later.

Organization Publications

Many organizations have newsletters or quarterly publications that keep employees abreast of the latest news and issues. Including program results in these publications can serve a number of purposes, including arousing general interest. A safety program may be evaluated to determine its impact on lost-time accidents. When the evaluation finds that the program does indeed impact lost-time accidents, an article can highlight these results. Stories about participants involved in a program and the results they achieve may help to generate interest in a program on the part of employees who would not otherwise have known about it. Reports of program success in organization publications can bring recognition to participants in the program. This public recognition can help to build confidence and self-esteem in the individuals highlighted.

Case Studies

The use of case studies is an effective way to communicate the results of a program evaluation. It is recommended that a few projects be developed in a case-study format. A typical case study describes the situation; provides appropriate background information, including the events that led to the program; presents the techniques and strategies used to develop the study; and highlights the key issues in the program and the evaluation.

Case studies can be used in group discussions, allowing interested individuals to react to the material, offer different perspectives, and draw conclusions about approaches or techniques. They can serve as self-teaching guides as individuals try to understand how evaluation is developed and used in the organization. They can also provide appropriate recognition for those who were involved in the actual case study or achieved the results.

The important issue is to understand which medium is most effective for the target audience and to include that decision in the overall communication strategy.

Communicate Results

The next step is the actual presentation of results. There are generally two issues to consider:

- Providing feedback

- Presenting results to senior management

Providing Feedback

The first issue is the feedback provided throughout the program being evaluated. This information is communicated primarily to the staff and project team. Feedback data provide information that suggests what immediate changes are necessary for continuous improvement.

Presenting Results to Senior Management

The second issue to consider concerns communication to senior management. Two questions that should be asked when planning communication to this group are "Do they believe you?" and "Can they take it?" If these two concerns are addressed at the outset, they are not as big an issue when it is time to present the final results.

In responding to the first question, "Do they believe you?" the key is to ensure that when a program reaps a very high ROI, the presentation of the results includes all of the steps covered in Table 19. Beginning with background information on the program and a description of the ROI Methodology will build credibility in the results and the evaluation process. Ensuring that the audience understands that efforts were made to be conservative in the evaluation will also build credibility. Also, reporting results in order beginning with Level 1, Reaction, and building up to Level 5, ROI, and intangible benefits will show senior management all of the elements that go into the ROI evaluation. If the ROI is presented up front, there is a risk that the audience will not hear the rest of the presentation. Their focus will be on the end results, not on the process.

The second question, "Can they take it?" refers to the fact that occasionally, a program may result in a less-than-desirable or even negative ROI. While no one wants a negative ROI, the ROI Methodology is not an individual performance evaluation—it is a process improvement tool. Negative ROIs can be invaluable sources of information on necessary changes and improvements—not only for the program being evaluated but for systems and processes supporting program implementation. In communicating low or negative ROIs, follow the same outline in Table 19. However, there should also be a plan for addressing the issues causing the negative ROI. If the program was too expensive, then acknowledge this and disclose a plan to reduce costs in the future. If the program was inappropriate for the problem being addressed, the needs assessment process may need to be adjusted. If there were barriers to implementing the skills learned and/or knowledge acquired during the program, identify those barriers and present them along with a solution for their removal. If the program proves to have been just plain ineffective, kill it and move on to something more useful to employees and the organization. The important point is to view low and negative ROIs as opportunities to make positive changes. When presenting these types of ROIs, be sure to present plans for improvement or next steps.

Analyze Reactions

The final step in the communication process is analyzing reactions to the communication. As with any process, evaluation of the communication is critical to understanding where improvements are necessary. Communication is probably one of the most critical areas, yet little emphasis is placed on its evaluation. Analyzing reactions to communication will allow for improvements in future reports, presentations, and other communication processes. It will allow for necessary changes in media or timing. It will help to ensure that the key issues for different target audiences are covered and that the results of ROI evaluations are clearly communicated to and understood by future audiences.

During the presentation of results, questions may be asked or the information challenged. This input is important to remember for the next program evaluation. Compiling the questions can be useful in determining what types of information should be included in future communication. Positive comments should also be noted.

Staff meetings are excellent forums for discussing reactions to the presentation of results. Comments can come from many sources, depending on the particular target audiences. When a major presentation on program results is made, a feedback questionnaire may also be used on the entire audience. The purpose of this questionnaire is to determine the extent to which the audience understood and believed the information presented. Another approach to measuring reactions to the presentation of results is to conduct a survey of the management group to determine their perception of training and performance improvement programs.

CHAPTER 5: SUCCESSFUL ROI IMPLEMENTATION

Although progress is being made in the widespread implementation of the ROI Methodology, there are still barriers that can inhibit implementation of the concept. Some of these barriers are realistic, while others are based on false perceptions. This chapter addresses these barriers and provides readers with potential next steps they can take to implement ROI successfully in their organizations.

Barriers to Implementation

The first step toward successful implementation of any process is to understand the potential barriers. Implementation of the ROI Methodology is no different. Founded or unfounded, these barriers are real and need to be addressed.

Costs and Time

A comprehensive measurement and evaluation process including ROI will add costs and time to a program's implementation, although the added amounts will likely not be excessive. The additional costs should be no more than 3–5 percent of the departmental budget. The additional investment in ROI should be offset by the results achieved from implementation (e.g., the elimination or prevention of unproductive or unprofitable programs). The cost/time barrier alone stops many ROI implementation plans early in the process. However, there are a few shortcuts and cost-saving approaches that can help to reduce the cost of the actual implementation shown in Table 19.

Table 19. Shortcuts to ROI Implementation

TIPS AND TECHNIQUES TO REDUCE THE COST OF IMPLEMENTING THE ROI PROCESS

- Build evaluation into the performance improvement process.

- Develop criteria for selecting program measurement levels.

- Plan early for evaluation.

- Share responsibilities for evaluation.

- Require participants to conduct major steps.

- Use shortcut methods for major steps.

- Use estimates.

- Develop internal capability.

- Streamline the reporting process.

- Utilize technology.

Source: Phillips, Patricia P. and Holly Burkett. 2001. *Managing Evaluation Shortcuts*. Infoline. Alexandria, VA: American Society for Training and Development.

Lack of Skills

Many staff members either do not understand ROI or do not have the skills necessary to apply the process within the scope of their responsibilities. Also, the typical program evaluation focuses more on qualitative feedback data than quantitative results. Consequently, a tremendous barrier to implementation is the discrepancy in the overall orientation, attitude, and skills of staff members engaged in program design, development, implementation, and evaluation. Some suggestions for building skills in ROI include the following:

- Attending public workshops

- Becoming certified in ROI implementation

- Conducting internal workshops

- Starting with less comprehensive evaluations and building toward more advanced projects

- Participating in evaluation and ROI networking forums

Faulty or Inadequate Initial Analysis

All too often inadequate analysis leads teams to the wrong conclusions, thereby leading them to the wrong solutions. Management requests to chase a popular fad or trend in the industry are often based on faulty analysis of the problem or opportunity. If a program is not necessary or not based on business needs, it may not produce enough benefits to overcome the costs. An ROI calculation for an unnecessary program will likely yield a negative value. To avoid offering an unnecessary or inappropriate program (which can lead to less than desired results), develop or enhance the performance consulting process. Become engaged with the client in order to gain a deeper understanding of their needs. This will help to ensure that the appropriate program or solution is implemented, yielding a greater ROI.

Fear

Some staff members do not pursue ROI because of fear of failure or fear of the unknown. Fear of failure appears in several ways. Some staff members will be concerned about the consequences of a negative ROI. They perceive the evaluation process as an individual performance evaluation rather than a process improvement tool. For others, a comprehensive measurement process can stir up the common fear of change and all of the unknowns that change brings. Although often based on unrealistic assumptions and a lack of knowledge of the process, fear is so strong that it becomes a real barrier to many ROI implementations. Making sure that staff members understand the process and its intent is key to dissolving this fear.

Discipline and Planning

Successful implementation of the ROI Methodology requires significant planning and a disciplined approach to keep the process on track. It requires implementation schedules, transition plans, evaluation targets, ROI analysis plans, measurement and evaluation policies, and follow-up schedules. The practitioner may not have enough discipline and determination to stay the course. This inevitably becomes a barrier, particularly if there is no immediate pressure to measure ROI. If clients or other executives are not demanding ROI evaluation, the staff may not allocate the time necessary for planning and coordination. Also, other pressures and priorities often eat into the time necessary for ROI implementation. Planning the work and working the plan are key to successful implementation.

False Assumptions

Many professionals have false assumptions about ROI that deter them from pursuing implementation. Some typical false assumptions are these:

- ROI can only be applied to a few narrowly focused programs.

- Senior managers do not want to see the results of programs expressed in monetary values.

- If clients do not ask for ROI, it should not be pursued.

- If the CEO does not ask for ROI, then he or she does not expect it.

While these assumptions are usually based on incorrect data or misunderstandings, they still form realistic barriers that impede the progress of ROI implementation. Again, understanding the methodology and the need for ROI are critical factors in overcoming this barrier.

Next Steps

Now that the ROI Methodology has been explained along with the various pieces of the evaluation puzzle, the question is, "What now?" How does one get started evaluating programs using the ROI Methodology? The previous section covering implementation issues provides some insight; as a focused review, Table 20 provides a checklist of steps to help newcomers to the ROI Methodology to begin the implementation process. As progress is made and issues surface, there are numerous resources available to assist in implementing ROI. Some of those resources are listed in the reference section at the back of this book.

Table 20. Next Steps

Implementing ROI

☐	Assess progress and readiness for ROI implementation.
☐	Organize a task force or network to initiate the process.
☐	Develop and publish a philosophy or mission statement concerning accountability and ROI for all programs.
☐	Clarify roles and responsibilities of project team members.
☐	Develop a transition plan detailing the steps necessary to implement ROI successfully.

☐ Set targets for evaluating programs at the various levels of evaluation.

☐ Develop guidelines to ensure that ROI is implemented completely and consistently.

☐ Build staff skills.

☐ Establish a management support system or champions of ROI.

☐ Enhance management support of and commitment to participation in the implementation of ROI.

☐ Achieve short-term results by evaluating one program at a time.

☐ Communicate results to selected audiences.

☐ Teach the process to others to enhance their understanding of ROI.

☐ Establish a quality review process to ensure that the evaluation process remains consistent and credible.

The Bottomline

So what is the bottomline on ROI? For generations, ROI has been used to show the value of programs, projects, and processes within organizations. The ROI calculation is the financial ratio used by accountants, chief financial officers, and executives to measure the return on all investments. The term ROI is already familiar to all executives and operational managers. It is not a new, fly-by-night catchphrase with an unknown meaning that can only be explained through elaborate presentations and is only understood in a very small area of an organization.

The ROI Methodology described in this book represents the use of the classic ROI economic indicator, yet goes beyond a cost-benefit comparison. It provides a balanced viewpoint of the impact of all types of programs, processes, and projects by taking into consideration participant reaction, learning, application of new skills and knowledge, and business impact achieved through the programs. The process presents the complete picture of program success. Furthermore, by including the critical step of isolating the effects of the program, the impact on business can be further linked to specific programs. The process presented in this book is based on sound research and conservative guidelines. Although not all programs should be evaluated at the ROI level, for those meeting specific criteria, ROI is a credible approach to providing evidence of a program's financial impact on an organization. A thorough and complete understanding of ROI can help to eliminate fears and overcome barriers to its implementation.

CHAPTER 6: FREQUENTLY ASKED QUESTIONS

Today's leaders must show accountability for the investments made in their programs and processes. Many leaders have found that actually measuring the ROI of a few selected, high-profile programs is an excellent way to show fiscal responsibility for key projects and initiatives. For almost two decades we at the ROI Institute have been assisting organizations with this important issue. In the past five years, we have kept track of the many questions that are often asked about ROI. These questions come from conferences and workshop participants, as well as clients with whom we work on consulting assignments. This chapter presents answers to the 25 most frequently asked questions about ROI.

1. **How does the ROI used in the context of program evaluation differ from the ROI used by the financial staff?**
    The classic definition of ROI is "earnings divided by the investment." In the context of calculating the ROI for programs such as learning and development, performance improvement, human resources, quality, marketing, etc., the earnings become the net benefits from the program (monetary benefits minus the costs), and the investment is the actual program cost. The challenge lies in developing the actual monetary benefits in a credible way.

2. **Do I have to learn finance and accounting principles to understand the ROI Methodology?**
    No—many of the principles of finance and accounting don't relate to what is needed to develop the return on investment in

programs such as those described in this book. However, it is important to understand issues such as revenue, profit, and cost. Ultimately, the payoff of programs and projects will be based on either direct cost savings or additional profit generated. It is helpful to understand the nature and types of costs and the different types of profits and profit margins.

3. **Do I have to know statistics to understand ROI?**
    Only very basic statistical processes are necessary to develop most ROI impact studies. It is rare for statistics to be needed beyond simple descriptive statistics. Sometimes hypothesis testing and correlations are necessary. These are simple concepts and are, by design, simplified as much as possible in the processes described in the book.

4. **Is ROI just one single number? How can you communicate a program's value with a number?**
    The ROI Methodology develops six types of data, with the actual ROI calculation being only one of them. The six types of data are these:

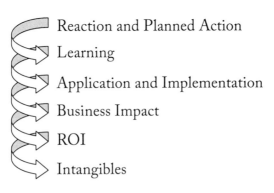

    Reaction and Planned Action
    Learning
    Application and Implementation
    Business Impact
    ROI
    Intangibles

5. **Aren't the levels of evaluation out of date and not applicable?**
    The original four levels developed by Don Kirkpatrick show how the data must be developed to generate value from a program. As shown above, the data are arranged in a chain of impact

that must exist if the learning, performance improvement, and human resources initiatives are to have business impact, which ultimately becomes business value. The chain of impact can be broken at any point; thus, correlations do not always exist between the levels, because there are barriers to success at any level. Although a few researchers take issue with the four levels, it is still the most widely used foundation for evaluation. ROI becomes the fifth level and is the consequence of the program expressed in monetary terms. These levels of results are applicable in all types of decision-making situations. A topic, content, or issue is presented, the audience reacts, acquires more information, applies (or does not apply) the information, and as a consequence some impact occurs. ROI (Level 5) brings in a new set of data—money—both in the numerator and the denominator. Because of the logic behind this chain of impact and the need for different types of data, the concept of levels is alive and well, and being implemented well beyond the learning, performance improvement, and human resources industries.

6. **Isn't ROI based on nothing but estimates that can be very subjective?**
   Estimates are used only when other methods are not readily available or become too time-consuming or expensive to obtain. When estimates are made, they are adjusted for the error of the estimate to improve their credibility. In essence, results are understated. Estimates, when necessary, are usually used in four areas:

   1. When records are not readily available to show the improvement or, in a forecast situation, where the data are unknown.
   2. When isolating the effects of a program.
   3. When converting data to monetary values.
   4. When calculating the costs (a widely accepted finance practice).

In every case, there are many alternatives to estimates and these alternatives are often recommended. Estimates are used routinely in some situations because they become the preferred method and are accepted by stakeholders, or they may be the only way to obtain the needed data.

7. **Isn't ROI too complicated for most non-technical professionals?**

The ROI calculation itself is a very simple calculation: net benefits divided by costs. The processes needed to arrive at the benefits follow a methodical step-by-step sequence, with guiding principles used along the way. The costs are developed using guidelines and principles as well. What complicates the process are the many options in each step in the process. The options are critical because of the various situations, programs, and projects that need to be evaluated and the different environments and settings in which they occur. Having standards to consider when selecting the options reduces the complication.

8. **Doesn't evaluation leading up to ROI cost too much?**

The cost for a study all the way through to ROI may represent as much as 5–10 percent of the budget for the entire program or project. This percentage varies considerably depending on the scope of the program or project. It is also important to note that in most organizations every program is evaluated at some level. The total cost of all evaluation, including selected ROI studies, is usually in the range of 3–5 percent of the total departmental budget.

9. **Is it possible to isolate the effects of my program from other factors?**

This is the most difficult and challenging issue, but it is *always* possible, even if estimates are used. Some of the most sophisticated and credible processes involve control groups, trend line analysis, and forecasting models. Other less sophisticated techniques are used, such as expert estimation and customer input. When estimates are used, the data should be adjusted for the error of the estimate. Always strive to carve out the amount of data directly related to the program or project.

10. Is it true that the ROI process does not reveal program weaknesses or strengths?

The ROI Methodology captures six types of data. At Levels 1, 2, and 3, data always captures deficiencies or weaknesses in the process. At Level 3, the process requires collecting data about the barriers to success and the enablers that increase success.

11. Is it true that the ROI process does not result in recommendations for improvement?

Each impact study using the ROI Methodology contains a section for recommendations for improvement. It is essential that this tool be utilized, first and foremost, as a process improvement tool. Recommendations for change are always appropriate, even when studies reflect a very successful project.

12. Is it appropriate to conduct an ROI study for every program?

Only a few select programs should be subjected to evaluation all the way through to the fifth level of evaluation (ROI). Ideal targets include programs that are very expensive, strategic, operationally focused, and highly visible, and those that involve large target audiences and have management attention in terms of their accountability. In most organizations using this methodology, only about 5–10 percent of the programs are selected for ROI analysis each year.

13. Which programs are <u>not</u> suited for ROI analysis (but may still achieve a positive ROI)?

Certain programs should not be evaluated all the way through to ROI. The following programs are not appropriate for ROI:

mandatory programs, compliance programs, legally required initiatives, specific operational job-related programs, brief programs, information-sharing programs, entry-level programs, new-to-the-job issues, and programs intended to align the individual with the organization.

14. **Who is using the ROI Methodology?**

Practically all types of organizations in the United States and around the world are using the ROI Methodology. To date, almost 4,000 private sector, public sector, and social sector organizations have formally implemented ROI through skill-building and ROI Certification. In essence, thousands of organizations are utilizing ROI Methodology through an informal implementation in various parts of their organization. In addition, almost 25,000 specialists and managers have taken either a one- or two-day ROI workshop, and more than 5,000 individuals have participated in five-day comprehensive certification workshops.

15. **What types of applications are typical for ROI analysis?**

The applications can vary, but usually include sales training, supervisory training, team building, executive development, competency systems, software utilization, leadership development, diversity, orientation systems, compensation and benefits, reward systems, skill-based pay, career management, major projects, meetings and events, communication strategies, and wellness initiatives. These topics make excellent targets for ROI Methodology as has been documented with case studies in the literature.

16. **How can I learn more about ROI?**

There are many options available to learn about ROI. Several books, case studies, and templates have been published, with many of them being published or made available through the

ROI Resource Center (www.roiresourcecenter.net). Additional resources are available through www.Amazon.com. In partnership with HRDQ, the publisher of this book, we are making available a kit that includes this book, a Participant Workbook, and a Facilitator Guide to assist organizations in developing fundamental skills. For those individuals who want to become proficient in the process, the ROI Institute offers a five-day certification workshop about 20 times a year. Additionally, on-site consulting and coaching is an option. For more information on these opportunities, visit www.roiinstitute.net.

17. **Can ROI be used on the front end of a project as a forecasting tool?**

ROI forecasting is an important part of the ROI Methodology. This process uses credible data and expert input and involves estimating the improvement (projected benefits) that will occur if a program is implemented. Projected benefits are compared to projected costs to develop the forecasted ROI.

18. **How does ROI compare to a balanced scorecard?**

The ROI process generates six types of data (reaction, learning, application, business impact, ROI, and intangibles) which comprise a scorecard. The Balanced Scorecard process developed by Kaplan and Norton (1996) suggests four categories of data (learning and growth, internal business processes, finance, and customer). The data generated with the ROI Methodology can all be grouped into one of these four categories. In addition, the ROI process adds two other capabilities not normally contained in the Balanced Scorecard methodology: it provides a technique to isolate the effects of a program, and it shows the costs versus benefits of a particular program or initiative. Thus, the ROI Methodology will complement the Balanced Scorecard process.

19. **How can I secure support for ROI in my organization?**

    Building support for the ROI Methodology is an important issue. Top executives will usually support the process when they realize the types of data that will be generated. Most of the resistance comes from those directly involved in programs, because they do not understand ROI and how it is to be used in the organization. Involving them in implementing the process and properly using data to drive improvements helps to lower the resistance. Efforts to implement any major change program will apply to the implementation of the ROI Methodology.

20. **How can I minimize staff resistance to the ROI Methodology?**

    Most staff will have some resistance to the ROI Methodology unless they see the value it can bring to their work. Involvement, education, and process improvement are key issues. It is often the fear of ROI that generates resistance—a fear based on misunderstandings about the process and how the data will be used. The ROI Methodology should be implemented as a process improvement tool and not as a performance evaluation tool for the staff. No one wants to develop a tool that will reflect unfavorably on their performance review. Improvement in key decisions about the use of ROI will help to minimize resistance. Also, resistance will be minimized when steps are taken to en-sure that the data are communicated properly, improvements are generated, and the data are not abused or misused.

21. **Should I conduct an ROI study on my own program?**

    If possible, the person evaluating the program should be inde-pendent of the program. It is important for the stakeholders to understand that the person conducting the study is objec-tive and removed from certain parts of the study, such as the data collection and the initial analysis. Sometimes these issues can be addressed in a partnering role or in limited outsourcing opportunities—whether data collection or analysis. In other situations, the issue must be addressed and the audience must understand that steps have been taken to ensure that the data were collected and analyzed objectively, and reported completely.

22. Are there any standards for ROI?

The ROI Methodology, as developed by Jack and Patti Phillips and their associates, contains standards labeled "Guiding Principles." (See page 34.) These provide consistency for the analysis with a conservative approach. The conservative approach builds credibility with the stakeholders.

23. What type of background is necessary for learning the ROI Methodology?

It is helpful for the individual to understand the business in which the studies will be developed. Knowledge about operations, products, and financial information is very helpful. Also, the individual should not have a fear of numbers. Although the ROI Methodology does not involve much statistical analysis, it does involve some data analysis. Excellent communication skills are needed to develop the various documents describing results and to present those results to a variety of stakeholder groups. Finally, the ability to partner with many individuals is extremely important. This requires much focus, contact, and collaboration with the client—this is a very client-focused methodology. The individual must be willing to meet with the key sponsors of programs and to build the relationships necessary to capture the data and communicate the data to them.

24. How is ROI on technology-enabled projects developed?

Applying the ROI Methodology to technology-enabled projects is the same as any other process, program, or solution. The monetary value of the benefits from the project is compared to the cost of the project. Many individuals assume that the benefits of a project remain the same and that only the costs to implement the project change due to the technology. While the costs of implementation may change, the benefits may change as well. An ROI study should be conducted to show the actual benefits of implementing the project, not just the cost savings achieved by changing approaches. For example, when an organization opts to implement technology-enabled learning versus in-person classroom training, the reason for doing so is often to reduce the cost of delivery. That cost savings shows up in the denominator of the equation, not in the numerator or the benefits side of the equation. The benefits derived from a technology-enabled training program are based on what people do with what they learn from the content of the program. The change to technology from classroom is a change in the delivery—but the content and the learning transfer strategy are the keys to gaining benefit and, ultimately, a positive ROI. So if the content design and delivery and the learning transfer strategy are weaker through the technology-enabled training than through the classroom training, a lower ROI is likely.

25. How do you calculate the ROI on the ROI?

This is a very good question to raise in terms of the payoff of using this methodology. The important issue is the value of implementing the process itself. While literally hundreds of organizations are reporting the benefits and successes, it is helpful to understand the internal payoff in the organization. The improvements and changes resulting from an impact study are tallied from one study to another and compared to the actual cost of the implementation. This, in essence, can generate the return on investment for utilizing this process. This approach is recommended for most major implementations.

REFERENCES

Alliger, G. M., and S. I. Tannenbaum. 1997. A meta-analysis of the relations among training criteria. *Personnel Psychology* 50, no. 2: 341–358.

American Productivity and Quality Center (APQC). 2000. *The corporate university: Measuring the impact of learning.* Houston: American Productivity & Quality Center.

ASTD. 2010. *State of the industry report.* Alexandria, VA: ASTD.

Benson, D. K., and V. P. Tran. 2002. Workforce development ROI. In *Measuring return on investment in the public sector.* Edited by P. P. Phillips. Alexandria, VA: American Society for Training and Development.

Broad, M. L., and J. W. Nestrom. 1992. *Transfer of training.* Boston: Perseus Books.

Friedlob, F. J. and G. T. Plewa. 1996. *Understanding return on investment.* San Francisco: John Wiley & Sons, Inc.

Horngren, C. T. 1982. *Cost accounting.* Englewood Cliffs, NJ: Prentice Hall.

Kearsley, G. 1982. *Costs, benefits, and productivity in training systems.* Reading, MA: Addison-Wesley Publishing.

Kirkpatrick, D. L. 1994. *Evaluating training programs: The four levels.* San Francisco: Berrett-Koehler Publishers.

Nas, T. F. 1996. *Cost-benefit analysis.* Thousand Oaks, CA: Sage Publications.

Phillips, J. J. 1995. Corporate training: Does it pay off? *William & Mary Business Review.* Summer: 6–10.

Phillips, J. J. 1996a. Was it the training? *Training and Development* (March).

Phillips, J. J. 1996b. How much is the training worth? *Training and Development* (April): 20–24.

Phillips, J. J. 1997a. *Return on investment in training and performance improvement programs.* Waltham, MA: Elsevier Butterworth-Heinemann.

Phillips, J. J. 1997b. *Handbook of training evaluation and measurement methods.* 3rd ed. Waltham, MA: Elsevier Butterworth-Heinemann.

Phillips, J. J. and P. P. Phillips. 2007. *Show me the money.* San Francisco: Berrett-Koehler.

Phillips, J. J. and P. P. Phillips. 2010. *Measuring for success: What CEOs really think about learning investments.* Alexandria, VA: ASTD.

Phillips, P. P. 2010. Calculating the return on investment. In *ASTD handbook of measuring and evaluating training.* Alexandria, VA: American Society for Training and Development.

Phillips, P.P., and H. Burkett. 2001. *Managing evaluation shortcuts.* Infoline. Alexandria, VA: American Society for Training and Development.

Schmidt, W. 1997. Cost-benefit analysis techniques for training investments. *Technical & Skills Training* (April): 18–21.

Sibbett, D. 1997. Harvard Business Review: 75 years of management ideas and practice 1922–1977. *Harvard Business Review.* Sep/Oct 1997 Supplement, 75:5.

Thompson, M. S. 1980. *Benefit-cost analysis for program evaluation.* Thousand Oaks, CA: Sage Publications.

Warr, P., C. Allan, and K. Birdi. 1999. Predicting three levels of training outcome. *Journal of Occupational and Organizational Psychology.* 72: 351–375.

ABOUT THE AUTHOR

Dr. Patti P. Phillips is President, CEO, and Co-Founder of the ROI Institute, Inc., the leading source of ROI competency building, implementation support, networking, and research. A renowned expert in measurement and evaluation, she helps organizations to implement the ROI Methodology in 35 countries around the world.

Since 1997, following a 13-year career in the electric utility industry, Phillips has embraced the ROI Methodology by committing herself to ongoing research and practice. Dr. Phillips has implemented ROI in private sector and public sector organizations. She has conducted ROI impact studies on programs such as leadership development, sales, new-hire orientation, human performance improvement, K-12 educator development, and educators' National Board Certification mentoring. Her current work includes research and application of the ROI Methodology in workforce development, community development, and social sector programs as well as corporate initiatives such as learning and development, human resources, and meetings and events.

Dr. Phillips teaches others to implement the ROI Methodology through the ROI Certification process, as a facilitator for ASTD's ROI and Measuring and Evaluating Learning Workshops, and as an adjunct professor for graduate-level evaluation courses. She serves on numerous doctoral dissertation committees, assisting students as they develop their own research on measurement, evaluation, and ROI.

Phillips speaks on the topic of ROI and accountability at conferences and symposia in countries around the world. She is often heard over the Internet as she presents the ROI Methodology to a wide variety of audiences via webcasts and podcasts.

A contributor to a variety of journals, Phillips, along with her husband, Jack Phillips, routinely authors, co-authors, and edits publications on the subject of accountability and ROI, including: *The Green Scorecard: Measuring the ROI in Sustainability Projects* (Nicholas-

Brealey, 2011); *ASTD Handbook of Measuring and Evaluating Training* (ASTD, 2010); *Beyond Learning Objectives* (ASTD, 2008); *Data Conversion* (Pfeiffer, 2008); *Beyond Learning Objectives* (ASTD, 2008); *Measurement and Evaluation Series* (Pfeiffer, 2008), which includes a six-book series on the ROI Methodology and a companion book of 14 best-practice case studies; *ROI Fundamentals* (Pfeiffer, 2008); *Return on Investment in Meetings and Events: Tools and Techniques to Measure the Success of All Types of Meetings and Events* (Elsevier, 2008); *Show Me the Money: How to Determine ROI in People, Projects, and Programs* (Berrett-Koehler, 2007); *The Value of Learning* (Pfeiffer, 2007); *Return on Investment Basics* (ASTD, 2005); *Proving the Value of HR: How and Why to Measure ROI* (SHRM, 2005); *ROI at Work* (ASTD, 2005); *Make Training Evaluation Work* (ASTD, 2004); *The Bottomline on ROI* (Center for Effective Performance, 2002), which won the 2003 ISPI Award of Excellence; the ASTD In Action casebooks *Measuring ROI in the Public Sector* (2002), *Retaining Your Best Employees* (2002), and *Measuring Return on Investment Vol. III* (2001); the ASTD Infoline series, including *Planning and Using Evaluation Data* (2003), *Managing Evaluation Shortcuts* (2001), and *Mastering ROI* (1998); and *The Human Resources Scorecard: Measuring Return on Investment* (Elsevier Butterworth-Heinemann, 2001).

Her academic accomplishments include a Ph.D. in International Development and a master's degree in Public and Private Management. She is certified in ROI evaluation and has been awarded the designations of Certified Professional in Learning and Performance and Certified Performance Technologist. Dr. Phillips can be reached at patti@roiinstitute.net, and you can follow her on Twitter at http://twitter.com/ppphillips.

ABOUT THE DEVELOPER OF
THE ROI METHODOLOGY

Dr. Jack J. Phillips is a world-renowned expert on accountability, measurement, and evaluation. Phillips provides consulting services for *Fortune* 500 companies and major global organizations. The author or editor of more than fifty books, he conducts workshops and presents at conferences throughout the world.

Phillips has received several awards for his books and work. On three occasions, *Meeting News* named him one of the 25 Most Influential People in the Meetings and Events Industry, based on his work on ROI. The Society for Human Resource Management presented him an award for one of his books and honored a Phillips ROI study with its highest award for creativity. The American Society for Training and Development gave him its highest award, Distinguished Contribution to Workplace Learning and Development, for his work on ROI.

His expertise in measurement and evaluation is based on more than 27 years of corporate experience in the aerospace, textile, metals, construction materials, and banking industries. Dr. Phillips has served as training and development manager at two Fortune 500 firms, as senior human resource officer at two firms, as president of a regional bank, and as management professor at a major state university.

Dr. Phillips regularly consults with clients in manufacturing, service, and government organizations in 52 countries including Australia and nations in North and South America, Europe, Africa, and Asia.

Phillips and his wife, Dr. Patti P. Phillips, recently served as authors for *The Green Scorecard: Measuring the ROI in Sustainability Projects* (Nicholas-Brealey, 2011) and series editors for the *Measurement and Evaluation Series* published by Pfeiffer (2008), which includes a six-book series on the ROI Methodology and a companion book of 14 best-practice case studies. Other books recently authored by Phillips include *The Consultant's Scorecard, 2nd edition: Tracking Results and*

Bottomline Impact on Consulting Projects (McGraw-Hill, 2010); *The Consultant's Guide to Results-Driven Proposals: How to Write Proposals that Forecast Impact and ROI* (McGraw-Hill, 2009); *ROI for Technology Projects: Measuring and Delivering Value* (Elsevier Butterworth-Heinemann, 2008); *Return on Investment in Meetings and Events: Tools and Techniques to Measure the Success of all Types of Meetings and Events* (Elsevier Butterworth-Heinemann, 2008); *Show Me the Money: How to Determine ROI in People, Projects, and Programs* (Berrett-Koehler, 2007); *The Value of Learning* (Pfeiffer, 2007); *How to Build a Successful Consulting Practice* (McGraw-Hill, 2006); *Investing in Your Company's Human Capital: Strategies to Avoid Spending Too Much or Too Little* (Amacom, 2005); *Proving the Value of HR: How and Why to Measure ROI* (SHRM, 2005); *The Leadership Scorecard* (Elsevier Butterworth-Heinemann, 2004); *Managing Talent Retention* (Pfeiffer, 2009); *Return on Investment in Training and Performance Improvement Programs*, 2nd ed. (Elsevier Butterworth-Heinemann, 2003); *The Project Management Scorecard* (Elsevier Butterworth-Heinemann, 2002); *Beyond Learning Objectives* (ASTD, 2008); *The Human Resources Scorecard: Measuring the Return on Investment* (Elsevier Butterworth-Heinemann, 2001); *Measuring for Success* (ASRD, 2010); and *The Consultant's Scorecard* (McGraw-Hill, 2000). Phillips served as series editor for ASTD's In Action casebook series, an ambitious publishing project featuring 30 titles. He currently serves as series editor for Elsevier Butterworth-Heinemann's Improving Human Performance series.

Dr. Phillips has undergraduate degrees in electrical engineering, physics, and mathematics; a master's degree in Decision Sciences from Georgia State University; and a Ph.D. in Human Resource Management from the University of Alabama. He has served on the boards of several private businesses and several nonprofits and associations including the American Society for Training and Development and the National Management Association. He is Chairman of the ROI Institute, Inc., and can be reached at (205) 678-8101, or by email at jack@roiinstitute.net.

PUT YOUR MONEY WHERE YOUR MOUTH IS

The Bottomline on ROI

For decades, senior leaders simply accepted learning and development as a necessary "people" cost. But today is different. Today, senior leaders are asking the questions that make some trainers cringe. They want to know what value training and development initiatives bring to the organization. They want to know the business impact, and they want to know the return on investment.

New from subject matter experts Jack Phillips and Patti Phillips, the *Bottomline on ROI* workshop complements this book and illustrates and reinforces the learning with real-world examples and exercises. Whether you are new to the ROI Methodology or are looking for ways to generate support for ROI within your organization, together these tools will provide you with a fundamental understanding of ROI and how it can be implemented.

Learning Outcomes

- Identify the benefits of developing ROI
- Learn how to assess an organization's readiness for ROI
- Understand the concept and assumptions of ROI
- Discover the criteria for effective ROI implementation
- Learn the ROI Methodology, a model that will produce a balanced set of measures
- Learn a communication process model for effective communication during the ROI process
- Discover how to get started implementing the ROI Methodology

The comprehensive Facilitator Guide includes easy-to-follow instructions for delivering a half-day, full-day, or two-day learning experience. The Participant Workbook comes complete with exercises, activities, quizzes, tools, and templates.

www.hrdqstore.com   800-633-4533
2002 Renaissance Boulevard, Suite 100, King of Prussia, PA 19406

ROI INSTITUTE™

ABOUT THE ROI INSTITUTE

The ROI Institute, Inc. is a leading resource on research, training, and networking for practitioners of the Phillips ROI Methodology.

With a combined 50 years of experience in measuring and evaluating training, human resources, technology, and quality programs and initiatives, founders and owners Jack J. Phillips, Ph.D., and Patti P. Phillips, Ph.D., are leading experts in return on investment (ROI).

The ROI Institute, founded in 1992, is a service-driven organization that strives to assist professionals in improving their programs and processes through the use of the ROI Methodology. Developed by Jack Phillips, this methodology is a critical tool for measuring and evaluating programs in 18 different applications in more than 40 countries.

The ROI Institute offers a variety of consulting services, learning opportunities, and publications. In addition, it conducts internal research activities for the organization, other enterprises, public sector entities, industries, and interest groups. Together with their team, Jack and Patti Phillips serve private and public sector organizations globally.

BUILD CAPABILITY IN THE ROI METHODOLOGY

The ROI Institute offers a variety of workshops to help you build capability in the ROI Methodology. Among the many workshops offered through the ROI Institute are:

- One-day *Bottomline on ROI* Workshop—provides the perfect introduction to all levels of measurement, including the most sophisticated level, ROI. Learn the key principles of the Phillips ROI Methodology and determine whether your organization is ready to implement the process.

- Two-day *ROI Competency Building* Workshop—the standard ROI Workshop on measurement and evaluation, this two-day program involves discussion of the ROI Methodology process, including data collection, isolation methods, data conversion, and more.

ROI CERTIFICATION™

The ROI Institute is the only organization offering certification in the exclusive Phillips ROI Methodology. Through the ROI Certification process, you can build expertise in implementing ROI evaluation and sustaining the measurement and evaluation process in your organization. Receive personalized coaching while conducting an impact study. When competencies in the ROI Methodology have been demonstrated, certification is awarded. There is not another process that provides access to the same level of expertise as our ROI Certification. To date, over 5,000 individuals have participated in this process.

For more information on these and other workshops, learning opportunities, consulting, and research, please visit us on the web at **www.roiinstitute.net**, or call us at **205.678.8101.**